Higher
Computing

Specimen Question Paper
2000 Exam
2001 Exam
2002 Exam
2003 Exam

© Scottish Qualifications Authority

All rights reserved. Copying prohibited. No part of this publication may be reproduced, stored in a retrieval system, or transmitted in any form or by any means, electronic, mechanical, photocopying, recording or otherwise.

First exam published in 1999.
Published by
Leckie & Leckie, 8 Whitehill Terrace, St. Andrews, Scotland KY16 8RN
tel: 01334 475656 fax: 01334 477392
enquiries@leckieandleckie.co.uk www.leckieandleckie.co.uk

Leckie & Leckie Project Team: Peter Dennis; John MacPherson; Bruce Ryan; Andrea Smith

ISBN 1-84372-120-1

A CIP Catalogue record for this book is available from the British Library.

Printed in Scotland by Scotprint.

Leckie & Leckie is a division of Granada Learning Limited, part of Granada plc.

Scotland's leading educational publishers

Introduction

Dear Student,

This past paper book provides you with the perfect opportunity to put into practice everything you should know in order to excel in your exams. The compilation of papers will expose you to an extensive range of questions and will provide you with a clear idea of what to expect in your own exam this summer.

The past papers represent an integral part of your revision: the questions test not only your subject knowledge and understanding but also the examinable skills that you should have acquired and developed throughout your course. The answer booklet at the back of the book will allow you to monitor your ability, see exactly what an examiner looks for to award full marks and will also enable you to identify areas for more concentrated revision. Make use too of the tips for revision and sitting your exam to ensure you perform to the best of your ability on the day.

Practice makes perfect. This book should prove an invaluable revision aid and will help you prepare to succeed.

Good luck!

Acknowledgements

Every effort has been made to trace the copyright holders and to obtain their permission for the use of copyright material. Leckie & Leckie will gladly receive information enabling them to rectify any error or omission in subsequent editions.

Pocket answer section for SQA Higher Computing SQP, 2000, 2001, 2002 and 2003

© 2003 Scottish Qualifications Authority, All Rights Reserved
Published by Leckie & Leckie Ltd, 8 Whitehill Terrace, St Andrews, Scotland, KY16 8RN
tel: 01334 475656, fax: 01334 477392, enquiries@leckieandleckie.co.uk, www.leckieandleckie.co.uk

Computing Higher Specimen Question Paper

Section I

1. Any valid complex condition
   Correct syntax for named software development environment eg COMAL, age>=15 AND age<18

2. *Three* stated from:
   consistent format; meaning full feedback; easy reversal eg undo; verification for destructive action; amount of info be memorised by user; good organisation of commands; help facilities; simple/meaningful commands; rapid assimilation; meaningful error messages; consistency of labels, abbreviation and codes; minimal input actions
   provision for multiple language levels

3. structured chart + example
   pseudocode + example
   data flow diagrams + example
   flowcharts + example

4. Valid description such as
   revisiting a stage in the SDP to modify it in the light of experience gained at a later stage

5. input validation
   find maximum

6. run-time-divide by zero; I/O errors eg file not found

7. find minimum
   comparing of times held in file to find min value

8. (a) (iii) 11111001
   (b) Real numbers are stored as mantissa and exponent

9. (a) A multi-scan monitor can operate at different refresh rates
   (b) (i) $5 \times 7 \times 600 \times 600 \times 1$ byte (1 260 000 bytes)
       (ii) 2 of High density (1·44 Mb) floppy disc, Zip disc, Hard disc drive CD-R, CD-RW
   (c) designed for the user;
       consistent display
       ease of use for non-expert
   (d) (i) hardware–network card
       (ii) topology–bus/star/ring with brief description

10. (a) Any valid COMMUNICATIONS protocol, eg FTP, http, X25
    (b) without protocols it would not be possible to ensure that all transmitted data was received and correctly interpreted by the receiving computer. The receiving computer must know what data formats, transmission speeds, etc were being used by the sending computer.

11. (a) *Any two valid pairs eg*:
       Prolog–AI
       Cobol–Commercial
       Pascal–Teaching programming
    (b) A brief description of such a use, eg Word Basic in MS Word
       A scripting language is used to create small programs, consisting of application commands, which can be used to automate certain processes and customise the application. For example, in a database a script could be written to perform a search, switch screen layouts and print a hard copy.

Section II

1. (a) *Any two of*:
      Compensate for different speeds
      Compensate for different data encoding
      Buffer data transfer
      Compensate for different signal characteristics
   (b) (i) larger RAM allows more programs/data to be held in memory, reducing the need for slower access to disks
       (ii) affected by interface bus width, rotation speed, bus speed
   (c) *Any two valid characteristics* **with** explanation of why they are important when considering a purchase, eg
       • Interface type—will affect speed of printing
       • print method—will affect quality of output and speed of printing
       etc
   (d) eg
       Scanner software—to capture images
       Authoring software—to construct presentation

Computing Higher
Specimen Question Paper (contd.)

2. (a) analysis
design
implementation
testing
evaluation
documentation

(b) **object**   **operation**
employee   digitise/adjust threshold/place etc
image
text   position/resize/etc
PIN   magnetically encode

(c) A reliable program will **consistently** operate without stopping due to design faults and will **consistently** produce correct outputs.

(d) (i) scanner or digital camera
(ii) $300 \times 300 \times 1$ inch => 90,000 pixels
256 greys = 8 bit depth, therefore each pixel requires 1 byte => 90,000 bytes

(e) voice print— microphone and sound card (hardware) voice recognition software
thumb print— scanner (hardware) image recognition software
any other valid security mechanism with accompanying hardware requirements

3. (a) Parameter passing reduces a module's dependency on global variables
Modules can therefore be reused **in other programs** without change

(b)

Module	Input	Output
1 Get stock identifier		Stock Identifier: integer
2 Get stock indicator	Stock Identifier: integer	Stock Indicator: integer
3 Update stock level	Stock Identifier, Stock Indicator: integer	Stocklevel: integer

(c) Bottom-up (test each module logic individually and integrate)
Top-down (test data flow and control with empty modules)

(d) It is likely that an **integer** will be represented in 16 bits.
Integers are usually represented in two's complement notation.
The largest value is $2^{15} - 1 = 32767$.
Accept also 65535 (if number assumed to be positive integer).

4. (a) Mark—integer value   Insert/centre
Result (formula)   Calculate
Total Passes (formula)   Calculate

(b) Eg Pascal
If ((Mark[1,1]>50) and ((Mark[1,2]>50) and ((Mark[1,3]>50)) then
eg Clarisworks Spreadsheet
And ((B2>0·5); ((C2>0·5); ((D2>0·5))

(c) eg Comparison based on HLL and GPP (Database) *Examples of valid points.*
Programming in a HLL would allow complete flexibility using the entire resources of the Operating System (GUI etc), whereas use of a GPP would only allow access to a limited subrange of features. Graphical features might be available, but mouse-over context sensitive help might not, in a GPP.
Input validation is possible in many GPPs, but tailored user feedback on errors would be easier to implement in a HLL.
On the other hand, learning time for a HLL is typically greater in a GPP.

(d) Set count to 0
For each student result do
    if result = 'pass' then
        add 1 to count
    end of if
end of loop

5. (a)
- manage User Interface
- manage Filing system
- manage memory allocation to applications/processes
- manage peripheral I/O

Accept component functions of these eg maintain FAT or similar. Accept references to file locking.

(b) (i) users expect to run multiple programs/ GUIs require multitasking to detect events
(ii) eg more sophisticated memory management, more sophisticated file handling

(c) User enters username and password
Data is encrypted and sent to server
Server validates against user database
Message sent from server to client machine to confirm or reject login

6. (a) *Two from*:
Calculated fields; reporting with subtotalling; screen layout design

(b) The field has been created as Text and not as a Date type this would result in a sort that is not in the expected order.

(c) **Advantage**
total flexibility of data structures, user interface, etc
Disadvantage
higher cost of production due to longer development cycle

6. **(continued)**
   (d) (i) Implementation stage
   (ii) Need to know whether data types and data structures can be supported in the *target* language.
   (e) The new system will use a different file format from the GPP. The old files can be converted to a standard file format such as comma separated values. This may be done by using an export function in the GPP. The CSV files can then be translated to the new file format.

Section III—Computer Programming

1. (a) Automatic line numbering in languages which require it
   Highlighting of keywords/reserved words eg making them bold or differently coloured
   Automatic layout of program structures, such as indenting the contents of a procedure or an IF structure.
   (b) (i) imperative language—Pascal, Cobol, Fortran
   (ii) declarative language—Prolog
   (iii) a language embedded in an application package—Word basic
   (iv) object oriented language—C++, Small talk
   (c) (i) Trace debugging tool allows inspection of variables and logical execution of code on a line by line basis
   (ii) Breakpoints—allow the program to be run normally, and to stop when the breakpoint is reached. Values of variables, stack etc are available for that point in the execution of the code
   (d) Trace facility on-line allows the tracking of values of variables, exits from procedures, transfer of control as the program is executed, giving information on screen as program is executed.
   Trace table—manual calculation of variable content at each stage of program execution. Relies on the programmer following the code exactly as a computer would do and calculating manually the variable values. Room for human error.

2. (a) *queue*—has a head (or front) and tail (or rear)
   items are added to the tail (enque) and removed from the head (de-que)
   this is a first in first out structure
   stack— has a top
   items are added to the top (push) and removed from the top (pop)
   this is a last in last out structure
   May refer to specific implementation or to related operations

62. **(continued)**
   (b) (checking value at top of stack, stack assumed to build from 0 up)
   if top of stack pointer = 0 then stack empty
   else item to be popped = item pointed to by top of stack pointer
   reduce top of stack pointer by 1
   end
   (c) Queue—"Job queue" **or** fill/empty a buffer **or** ...
   Stack—store return address when a subroutine is called **or** parsing arithmetic expressions
   (d) Linear search can be applied to any list structure
   Binary search requires items to be in order and addressable
   Binary search is more efficient, but could only be applied to a file if the criteria were satisfied

3. (a) (i) record structure with components for each item of date
   text (string) of ASCII characters
   integer—numerical offset from some reference date
   (ii) eg record vs string : strings could not be compared for alphabetical order because of the structure required so would have to be converted to another form, whereas records could be compared by year then month then day.
   (b) (i) The records must be stored in alphabetical order of surname
   The list structure must be addressable (ie array rather than linked list)
   (ii) set lower pointer to 0
   set upper pointer to size of list
   ask for name to be searched for
   repeat
      determine midpoint of list ((upper + lower)/2)
      if name at midpoint = name to be searched for then name found
      else if upper pointer < lower pointer entire list has been searched
      else if name at midpoint < name to be searched for set lower pointer to midpoint + 1
      else
         set upper pointer to midpoint − 1
   end of repeat when name found or entire list has been searched
   (c) eg bubblesort, quicksort
   Bubblesort is economical of memory but may require much processor time
   Quicksort requires less processor time on average, but is very demanding of memory

Computing Higher
Specimen Question Paper (contd.)

4. (a) eg Using Pascal
    Type
    Student List = ARRAY [1..40][1..9] of integer;
    Type
    Student Rec = RECORD
            Student ID : integer;
            Test Results : ARRAY [1.8] of integer;
        END;
    Student List = Array [1..40] of Student Rec;

   (b) Array of records, because it uses **sensible identifiers** to represent the different components of each record.

   (c) Set total mark to zero, set number of tests to zero
    For each of the test marks
        If the mark is valid
            Add mark to total mark
            Add 1 to number of tests
        End if
    End for
    Calculate average
    If number of tests is less than 6 then
        Set grade to 7
    Else
        Case average of
            0 – 39   Set grade to 6
            40 – 49   Set grade to 5
            50 – 59   Set grade to 4
            60 – 69   Set grade to 3
            70 – 79   Set grade to 2
            80 –100   Set grade to 1
        end case
    end if

   (d) eg
    Writing the two dimensional array could require a nested FOR loop to write the individual integers, while
    Writing the records would require a simple loop
    So the Record representation would require less write-to-file operations and would be more efficient

Section III—Artificial Intelligence

1. (a) **Knowledge Base**—the special knowledge stored here written in a knowledge representation language eg rules or frames + database
    Inference Engine—reasoning part. The IE determined which question to ask the user in which order, then matches the users answers with the KB
    Explanatory Interface—(user interface) communicate with the user. Must ask the user appropriate questions in an easy manner and explain why question asked and how answer obtained

1. (continued)
   (b) (i) using a certainty factor
       (ii) To represent this knowledge as a fact
            has_condition (orange marsh fever, orange, weak, high temperature)
       (iii) The software must be tested
             The software must be evaluated
       (iv) ADVISE 25 mg orthomyolite three times daily
            IF patient_age>=16 AND patient_age<=70
            AND disease is Orange March Fever
            ADVISE 15 mg orthomyolite three times daily
            IF patient_age<16 OR patient_age>70
            AND disease is Orange March Fever

2. (a) (i) as a set of facts and rules
       (ii) programs in declarative languages require a description of the problem rather than a method of solution, as in imperative languages
            In AI, problems tend to suit being described rather than being solved by a predetermined list of instructions

   (b) (i) a human would expect the names edinburgh and london in the responses but the program as written will not return this
       (ii) is_in (x z) if is_in (x y) and is_in (y z)

   (c) Attempts to use rule 12, instantiating Y to pound and X to scotland,
    but fails as there is no corresponding currency() rule
    Attempts to use rule 13, so attempts to satisfy sub-goals
    •is_in() is satisfied by rule 6
    •can_use–attempts rule 12 again
    Subgoal currency() succeeds at rule 11
    So the query succeed

   (d) Solution to rules 11 and 12 without NOT are x=UK, edinburgh, scotland, england, and these solutions would simply be negated by the NOT.
    If you wanted to establish which places you could not use the pound you would need a new rule.

3. (a) Eg Visual identification of objects
       Deductive reasoning (eg diagnosis)

   (b) Speech recognition—the sound of a spoken word is matched to its corresponding written word. This does not necessarily require the computer to attach a meaning to that word
    Natural Language Processing—analysing a sequence of words in order to determine the meaning of the words (semantic analysis)

3. **(continued)**

   (c) eg automated translation between human languages
   Where rather than just translate word by word, the meaning of whole phrases and sentences is translated

   (d) Words with more than one meaning (record)
   Words which can be more than one part of speech (bearing)

   (e) Parallel Processing
   Use of more than one processor to process task
   Each task is divided into discrete subtasks which may be allocated to separate processors
   Speeds up either computer vision or neural networks

4. (a) person identification

   (b) speech recognition

   (c) Pattern recognition requires a large database of references to be searched quickly.
   Insufficient RAM will reduce the size of the database which can be searched
   Insufficient processor speed (or throughput()) will reduce the rate at which the database can be searched

   (d) Input data can differ from what is stored in the database, eg an object may be viewed from a different angle.
   Depending on the programming of the pattern recognition system, the object may not be recognised.

   (e)
   - A brute force method would carry out an exhaustive search
   - Trying to match, pixel by pixel, the search item against every image in the database
   - Heuristics attempt to cut down the search by applying a rule of thumb
   - Quickly reduce comparisons—in this example you might count the colour codes of the source and target quickly eliminate mismatches and avoid further in-depth image comparisons.

Section III—Computer Networking

1. (a) **Bus:**
   Advantages
   - easy to attach new nodes at any point of cable
   - cheaper than other options
   - one node out of action doesn't affect the rest of the network

   Disadvantages
   - common cable—if it breaks, channel failure, whole network doesn't work
   - single collision zone may reduce overall bandwidth

4. (a) **(continued)**
   Star
   Advantages
   - all links connect directly to central node
   - high overall bandwidth possible depending on central node type

   Disadvantages
   - entire network is dependent on the central node working
   - if line goes down only one node affected, but if central node fails, whole network will fail
   - higher cabling costs

   (b) (i) transfer of data between two (or more) networks involving change of protocols

       (ii) up to date information on the most recent research
       communication with other practitioners to exchange ideas

   (c) Video conferencing is the live connection of two or more people (at different sites) using computer networks to transmit audio and video data
   Hardware—each participant has a video camera, microphone and speakers mounted on their computer. As the two participants speak to one another, their voices are carried over the network and delivered to the other's speakers and whatever images appear in front of the camera appear in a window on the other participant's monitor. To overcome the bandwidth and latency limitations of current networks, video compression is often used. ISDN is a set of protocol and interface standards that effectively constitute an integrated (voice, video and data) telephone network. These standards promote global availability and compatibility of ISDN products and services. JPEG compression of still pictures; MPEG compression and storage of moving pictures

   (d) *point-to-point*—data is transmitted directly to receiver. Little interference. Speed of data transfer since in real time. Require little delay
   internet—transfer not direct so time delay.

2. (a) A network of interconnected networks organised so that communication is possible

   (b) Router (but allow gateway)

   (c) (i)
   - standards allow signals to be interpreted in the same way at sender and receiver, allowing standard hardware to be used
   - standards allow data/messages to be interpreted the same way at sender and receiver

Computing Higher Specimen Question Paper (contd.)

2. (c) (continued)

    (ii)
- not using standards might give greater security as signals would not be recognised
- not using standards allows the tailoring of transmission characteristics to one's own data transmission needs

(d) (i) Transport layer provides two-way, reliable, cost effective, end to end exchange of data; may involve multiplexing and re-sizing of blocks. Flow control and sequencing of the data blocks is performed at this level.

(ii) Network layer takes packet-sized data blocks from the transport level and maps the addresses to network addresses. If routing required, then responsibility for this is also taken here.

3. (a) **Advantages**
- reduced cost (no wide area communications costs, no modems required, no subscriptions necessary)
- dedicated pages of information may be set up
- valuable time not wasted browsing unnecessarily
- no external security threats

Disadvantages
- information may be too restricted
- not as up to date as Internet
- lack of communication in a global market

Allow some latitude in expression. Other valid answers possible. Points must be non-trivial.

(b) Network operating system controls the processes of communication between the host computers, all of which may be very different from one another.

(c) (i) *peer to peer network*
simple networking strategy, not involving a dedicated server where any station can make its resources available to the rest of the stations on the network

(ii) *client/server*
stations do not have equal status—it is either a client or a server; the user (client) is allocated privileges which permit/deny access to certain resources. The server contains info of user IDs and privileges

3. (c) (continued)

(iii) *distributed processing* refers to a variety of systems that use more than one computer or processor to run an application. A LAN may be designed so that a single program can run simultaneously at various sites. Most distributed processing systems contain sophisticated software that detect idle CPUs on the network and parcels out programs to utilise them

(d) **For**
E-mails can seem more abrupt and rude than intended as recipient cannot see body language or hear the tone of the sender.

Automated responses give the illusion of a fast reply but in reality mean that a request is often forgotten about.

Against
The use of video conferencing allows face to face communication across vast distances which increases human contact.

The use of e-mail and file transfer allows families to keep in touch with relatives who live far away in a way which is much more immediate than by using normal mail.

4. (a) Expect answers in terms of packet filtering types of firewall, wide variety of responses possible. Typical units of response will include:
- firewall computer will only transfer packets for particular ports
- firewall computer may accept/reject packets from certain IP addresses
- firewall rules may force client computers to route traffic via more secure "bastion hosts"

Annotated diagrams are acceptable.

(b) The URL describes
- the transfer protocol, in this case ftp
- the name of the remote host, in this case ftp.somesite.sch.uk
- the file or resource on the remote computer, in this case names.doc

(c) It is not expected that the actual codes used by the ftp client and server programs would be used, but correct listing of these would be acceptable.
- connection is established between the two computers
- the transfer protocols, eg binary or text transfer, are established
- the existence and permissions of the requested file are verified
- the file is transferred in small chunks, each chunk is acknowledged
- completion of transfer is acknowledged and the connection is terminated

Section III—Multimedia Technology

1. Mention of:
   Pits and Lands
   Spiral arrangement with sectors in sequence (or single track ...)
   Sectors of 2048 bytes
   Mapped by software to 512 byte sectors
   ECC code after each sector to help protect data against corruption

2. (a) Contrast on original image is actually poor (eg pencil drawing)
   Threshold value set wrongly in scanning software

   (b) Similar looking characters confused
   Software attempts to interpret graphics as text
   Software fails to interpret text layout correctly (eg columns not recognised)
   failure to recognise words in different language

3. Eg
   Kerning; control of positioning of images/text to very fine tolerances; Text wrap around graphics; Image cropping; colour separation of output

4. The process seeks to avoid "blobs" of black and white corresponding to colours in images.
   Images are analysed for colour and intensity/texture.
   A range of half tone patterns is substituted for these colours/textures in the output image by the printing software.

5. • Min 15" Video display, 640X480 pixels in 16 bit colour, with hardware acceleration
   • 200 mHz Pentium with hardware assisted MPEG1 capability
   • Minimum RAM 64MB to support speech recognition
   • Hard Disk space 1GB
   • Sound Card output quality, 44.1 kHz, 16 bit sampling rate

6. (a) JPEG best for photographic type images
   GIF best for images with little colour gradient (eg cartoons)

   (b) **GIF**
   Repeating patterns of pixels are identified. One copy stored in a table and then referred to in compressed file. File size is reduced but no information is lost. Lossless compression.

   JPEG
   Known limitations of human vision are used to remove information which will not unduly affect the perceived quality of the image. File size is reduced by removing information. Lossy compression.

   (c) Note that the question refers to storage of data in files
   MIDI—sequence of descriptions of each note, with values for each characteristic
   One value identifies separate channel for each instrument
   Information for generating sounds of different instruments held in separate library file
   Digitised sound—sequence of values (pairs of values if in stereo) Each value is a sample of the total sound for a small, constant interval of time
   Typically 16 bits per channel, with sample rates around 22 or 44 kHz

   (d) • audio tape is input via sound card line input
   • digitised to AIFF format file—each track is a separate file
   • CD-R software used to generate audio CD, one file per track with separators

7. (a) **video**
   storage requirements—100 ppi, 40 ppcm
   $5 \times 5 = 25 \times 1600 = 40\,000$ pixels $\times 24 = 120$ kbytes per uncompressed frame

   data representation—MPEG 1 (i-frames, p-frames and b-frames)

   input methods—digital camcorder delivers MPEG bitstream (eg Firewire) OR camcorder + video card + MPEG encoder (might be on card)

   animated sequence
   storage requirements—see above
   data representation—Quicktime
   input methods—via some art package, and assembled in eg Macromedia Director

   (b) animation which consists of large areas of flat colour, but uses relatively small numbers of colours could be designed much more clearly than live video which could be visually noisy and messy (compression artefacts).
   This would make it easier for the user to assimilate information.
   Small videos on a low-resolution monitor do not look very good.

   (c) • 3D modeller
   • 3D renderer to generate image frames (GIF, TIFF)
   • Put into Director as cast members to generate image sequence (quicktime)
   Select MPEG for 3D-image output from Director

Computing Higher 2000

Section I

1. (a) **Reliable**—Program will run without stopping due to design faults. / Program will produce expected results on every occasion

    Maintainable—Program can be changed easily in order to correct errors or add extra functions. *(A list of attributes of a maintainable program is acceptable)*

    Fit for Purpose—Program meets the specification

    (b) *One of*

    A specification has a formal structure, whereas a problem description has not.

    A specification is unambiguous whereas a problem description may require clarification.

    A specification is a precise statement of the inputs to a program, the processes which will be carried out and the outputs from the program.

    A specification is a legally binding contract whereas a problem description is not.

2. (a) **Student Mark**—Integer

    Student Grade—Character *(or String or Text)*

    Accept descriptions of structured data types which represent lists of either or both of these

    (b) *Two from*

    Editor—Used to enter and amend program statements/text.

    Error Tracing Tools—To help locate the source of errors in program code.

    Compiler—translates entire source code into object/machine code.

    Interpreter—translates source code at run time, line at a time.

    (c) (iii) Input validation

3. (a) **Analysis**—Clarifying and understanding the problem and converting a rough outline of the problem into a precise problem specification

    (b) Interviewing the clients.

    Observing existing system and making observation notes.

    Gathering/inspecting information sources/existing documentation.

    The WHAT, WHERE, WHEN, WHY, WHO system.

4. **As a bit map.** The complete image is represented by a grid of pixels. Each pixel is assigned a number which represents its colour or tone. This number is stored in memory.

    As a set of object definitions (or vectors). *(In this case an ellipse, a line and a text object.)* Each object is represented by a set of object attributes. For example a line may be described by its starting point, length and thickness. The values of the object attributes are stored in memory.

5. **Bus width**—Increasing bus width increases data throughput per cycle

    Use of caches to speed up transfer of data between memory and processor.

    Pipelining

6. *Any **two** valid OS functions for this purpose including eg*

    Locating file on fileserver volume (ie verifying existence).

    Checking access rights.

    Checking availability of memory and allocating memory to file. *(Strictly allocating I/O buffer space)*

    Transferring file from fileserver volume to memory.

7. (a) **Control Unit**—causes instructions to be Fetched, decoded and executed **or** manages the INTERNAL operation of the processor.

    (b) *Any **two** from*:

    Clock (provides timing signal to allow synchronisation of processor and bus operations),

    Interrupt (to signal an asynchronous hardware event),

    Read, Write

    (c) Storage locations within the processor *(accept descriptions such as "can be used for storing instruction while it is being decoded", "storing data which is required for a calculation or storing the address of the next instruction")*.

8. *Any **two** from:*
    Name of module,
    Description of module's function
    Parameters required by module,
    Limitations or known bugs.

9. (a) • Typically a "higher level" programming language or 4GL, eg a SORT command may be available.
    Each command may carry out complex operations which would require many lines of code if implemented in a high level language.
    • Data items match those of corresponding GPP
    • Operations match those of corresponding GPP

9. (continued)

(b) Any valid example which involves combining a series of application functions eg perform a search on a database, load a form letter and perform a mailmerge, *but not just a description of a function which is standard in the particular package.*

Section II

1. (a) (i) Number of pixels = 3 × 1200 × 1·5 × 1200 = 6 480 000
   8 bits per pixel so each pixel requires 1 byte
   Storage Requirements = 6 480 000 bytes (6328 K = 6·18 M)

   (ii) Hard disk/also: *Jaz cartridge/DVD Ram/MO disc/WORM*. Over 600 M capacity required and random access required.

   (b) (i) The colour of a pixel is represented by a 24 bit number. This should allow 2^{24} colours.

   (ii) The image is to be displayed on a monitor which is only capable of around 72 dpi.
   The higher resolution of the image will not be shown on this device/the displayed image will have to be calculated from the stored image.
   If the image resolution was reduced to 72 dpi, storage requirements would be reduced with no reduction in the quality of the displayed image.

   (c) (i) **Multimedia Authoring Package.** Each property description layed out on a screen or card. Menu card uses buttons to link to required property.

   (ii) **Advantage**—More interesting presentation. Sound and animations possible.
   Disadvantage—It would not be possible to (or at least not so easy to) search for suitable properties.

2. (a) Faster implementation as coding to create and manipulate data structures already exist.
   Only require to create data files and customise the interface.
   More reliable as underlying application package has already been tested for errors.

   (b) (i) **macro**—a sequence of instructions which has been stored and can be executed by issuing a single instruction

   (ii) **creation of student details**—create macro to store commands (or menu selections) to select the correct input screen format (or layout) and create a blank record
   OR
   updating of student details—create macro to store commands to select search screen format, accept input into search field, carry out search
   Similar for printing of personalised reports and students results summary.

   (c) **corrective maintenance**—to correct errors in the program which were not detected during testing
   perfective maintenance—to add extra functions which have been requested by the user

   (d) Basic level of access allows users to see data. Even this is password protected ensuring privacy of data.
   Only authorised staff will be given access to update records ensuring that data is accurate.

3. (a) **event driven**—no start/end point; executes certain portions of code when an event happens, such as a button being selected
   declarative—search based (depth first/breadth first) based on previously defined rules / facts, pattern match to find solution
   procedural—executes program in sequence, executing one step at a time; control structures (loops) can be easily repeated

   (b) Creating an interactive tutor for children where selecting different objects causes different parts of the program to be executed.
   Reasons: Not possible to determine in advance the order in which objects will be chosen. Programmer can concentrate on programming each event handler without worrying about how to link them together.

   (c) data sent bit by bit along a single "wire"/data line
   whereas in parallel date transmission many bits are sent simultaneously along several "wires"

   (d) *Any **two** of*:
   changing voltage levels
   status information
   device selection
   controls signals
   data storage/buffering,
   (brief descriptions required)

4. (a) cpu executes a sequence of instructions which are stored in memory

   (b) *Any **two** of*:
   simpler arithmetic, less chance of signal degradation, easily implemented in digital electronics . . .

   (c) fetch instruction from memory
   increment program counter
   decode instruction
   execute instruction

Computing Higher 2000 (contd.)

4. (continued)

   (d) **Address bus increase**—increase in *possible* memory capacity of system

   Data bus increase—increase in data throughput per machine cycle

   (e) a GUI requires more data processing than a command-driven interface,
   so would require wider data bus (for speed) and larger addressable memory (large data structures associated with GUI) but is seen as desirable

   WHEREAS a processor with smaller address and data buses (eg an 8Bit processor) could not support these features and would require the developer to choose a command or character menu based HCI

5. (a) (i) the data that the program must be able to handle is part of the specification
   test schedule clarifies understanding of problem

   (ii) normal, extreme, exceptional

   (b) (i) **local variables**—subprogram does not alter any variables in other subprograms

   parameter passing—subprograms can be used in different programs without having to rename variables

   (ii) so that it can be re-used in other programs

   (c) Eg the problem can be sub-divided into independent sub-problems and distributed; different members of the team can work on these simultaneously, thus reducing overall development time
   parameter passing between modules allows programmers to work independently without their code interfering with others

   (d) (i) **Advantage**
   floppy drives are (nearly) universal

   Disadvantage
   many discs required (1·4 Mb maximum per disc)

   (ii) **Advantage**
   all fits on 1CD

   Disadvantage
   not everyone has access to CD drive/relative difficulty of CD manufacture

6. (a) leading 0 would be lost if stored as a number

   (b) Calculate the total cost of order:
   ISBN number—array of strings—value
   total cost—real—reference

   Determine discount:
   total cost—real—value
   no of high value books—integer—value

   (c) eg
   IF (no of high value books>=3) AND (total cost>250) THEN give 5% discount

   (d) conditional loop (accept REPEAT Until, WHILE DO or similar)
   the number of books in the list is not known in advance

   (e) Both modules involve linear traverse of same data structure
   Both sets of code could be incorporated in a single loop without loss of correctness, reducing processor overhead

Section III—Computer Programming

1. (a) purpose of editor is to allow for creation and amendment of source code
   purpose of debugger is to allow for detection of errors in source code
   stage of editing—implementation
   stage of debugging—testing (accept maintenance since perfective maintenance requires debugging)

   (b) automatic indentation of program statements
   automatic line numbering
   highlighting source keywords

   (c) (i) Description of structured walkthrough of source code

   (ii) *Any **two** of the following*:
   trace facility to track values of variables and parameters
   breakpoints to examine values of variables at specified point in execution
   ability to step through program execution one source line at a time

   (d) (i) possible errors are fed back as each line of source code is interpreted
   programmer alerted to program line source of error making correction potentially faster

   (ii) compiler generates separate error report file listing all errors detected within the program source

2. (a) stack places most recent item at top of structure
   last item in will be first item out
   needs to maintain a pointer to the top of the stack
   queue places the most recent item at the tail end of the structure
   first item in will be the first item out
   needs to maintain a pointer to the head and tail of the structure

2. (continued)

   (b) **POP from STACK**
   if stack is not empty then
   set data out to be item in position identified
   by top of stack pointer
   decrement top of stack pointer

   PUSH onto STACK
   if stack is not full then
      increment top of stack pointer
      put data item into position identified by
      top of stack pointer

   Top of stack must be incremented **before** an item is added or the previous last item will be overwritten

   (c) (i) operates on an ordered list
   repeatedly divides the list in half
   eliminating upper or lower section of
   list depending upon result of
   comparison of midpoint with target
   until target is found or search is
   exhausted

   (ii) To find the number 40 in the list 20 30 40 50 60 70

   Binary Sort would require 1 comparison
   Linear Sort would require 3 comparisons

3. (a) *Many possible variations of languages.* eg in Pascal
   Two D Array
   var tiles : array[1..4,1..4] of integer;
   or
   const
      tilerow = 4;
      tilecol = 4;
   type
      tiles = array[1..tilerow, 1..tilecol] of integer
   Record
   type board = record
          tile1, tile2, tile3, tile4, tile5,
          tile6, tile7 . . . tile16 : integer,
          end;
   One D arrays in parallel:
      tilerow1:array[1..4] of integer;
      tilerow2:array[1..4] of integer;
      tilerow3:array[1..4] of integer;
      tilerow4:array[1..4] of integer;

   (b) procedures   PROCEDURE
   meaningful variable
   names   VAR exponential : real
   internal commentary {this is a comment}

   (c) TILES[1.1]:=10;
   TILES[1.2]:=15;
   TILES[1.3]:=3;
   etc
   RECORD
   WITH TILES DO
     BEGIN
        tile1 := 10; tile2 := 15; tile3 := 3; etc
     END

ONE DIMENSIONAL ARRAYS IN PARALLEL
TILEROW1[1] :=10;
TILEROW1[2] :=15;
TILEROW1[3] :=3;
etc

4. (a) End of a word detected by a space character or a full stop

   (b) for rowloop = 1 to rowmax do
      for colloop = 1 to colmax do
         if arrayelement[rowloop,colloop] = target value then
            increment occurrence count
         end of if
      end of loop (colloop)
   end of loop (rowloop)

   (c) Method must ensure that all array elements are used to store words ie no gaps. This means that information about which line a word is on must be stored alongside it OR the end of a line must be represented by a code which is stored in the array next to the last word in that line.

   Possible solutions:
   - 1D array of strings where each word is stored in its own array element. An end of line character (or word) is stored in its own array element after the last word in that line
   - The line number of each word is tagged on to the end of the word and stored in the same array element as that word
   - Use a separate list of pointers telling where corresponding lines start in the array

   (d) (i) **systematic testing**—to test in a structured manner (top-down/bottom-up)

   comprehensive testing—to provide test cases that provides for normal extreme and exceptional testing

   (ii) systematic testing allows the programmer to test small parts in isolation which are then integrated to verify data flows. This narrows the focus of detecting and removing errors resulting in software that is more robust

   comprehensive testing ensures that the logic of the program is tested exhaustively. This results in more robust software

Computing Higher 2000 (contd.)

Section III—Artificial Intelligence

1. (a) (i) provide advice/information in a limited area of expertise
   (ii) to increase user confidence or to provide user with reasoning which led to the advice
   (b) IF food is meat AND has sharp teeth
   THEN Eustreptospondylus
   IF food is meat AND has powerful jaws
   THEN Tyrannosaurus Rex
   IF food is plants AND has a beak like mouth
   THEN Multaburrasaurus
   (or similar)
   (c) (i) appropriate diagrams or descriptions
   depth-first follows one branch to its end before trying the next branch breadth-first tests all nodes at one level before moving to next level
   (ii) **Advantage:**
   uses less memory
   Disadvantage:
   may never find a solution, or the best solution

2. (a) (i) no
   (ii) looks for a matching clause, finds clause 11, X=kirsten, Y=theseeker
   first subgoal is film (theseeker Z)
   finds match at clause 9, Z=12
   second subgoal is persons_age(kirsten W)
   finds match at clause 1, W=12
   3rd subgoal is 12>=12 which succeeds
   (b) (i) following similar logic to the above, would lead to evaluation of 6>=U which fails
   (ii) replace U with 0 (anyone over the age of 0 can watch a U)
   or replace with a rule like can_see (X Y) if film (Y u)
   (c) (i) features (theseeker animals)
   (ii) is_suggested_for (P Q R) if can_see (Q P) and features (P R)

3. (a) system must be taught to recognise typical re-usable and reject tins
   visual input then compared against these stored patterns
   (b) deformation may be hidden
   may be some other reason for rejecting tins
   (c) (i) heuristics = "rules of thumb"—things which are usually true
   (ii) common types of deformation could be identified, with a "rule of thumb" about which should be rejected
   (iii) endless possibilities—likely answers might include chess moves (if possible, take high value pieces)
   (d) parallel processing with brief description eg increase processing throughput by dividing task into subtasks spread across multiple processors
   neural networks with brief description

4. (a) (i) developing an "intelligent" machine which would pass the Turing test
   (ii) knowledge representation
   (iii) limited domains—expert systems, vision . . .
   (b) Short description of Turing test
   user at terminal connected electronically to human or program at other side of wall
   if user can't tell which, the program has passed the test
   (c) (i) computer to be able to respond intelligently/interpret purposefully to input in the form of human language (written or spoken)
   (ii) 1 mark for any valid application
   1 mark for how NLP is used within the application
   eg application might be as an interface to a database system allowing users to enter requests in natural language. This would be analysed and translated into a formal command which could be carried out by the database
   (iii) any 2 distinct points (eg words with multiple meanings/parts of speech, incorrect syntax, dialect/foreign/ technical words)

Section III—Computer Networking

1. (a) sharing of resources (printers, scanners . . .) access to shared data
   (b) **bus**—no new hardware (switches, hubs . . .)
   star—more flexible and extendible, less affected by cable failure
   (c) (i) router
   (ii) routes appropriate packets from LAN to WAN, transfers WAN packets onto LAN
   (d) (i) HTTP is a communications protocol governing the transfer of hypertext data
   HTML is a programming/markup language defining how the content of hypertext data should appear
   (ii) eg
   http://www.tannafordhigh.sch.uk/homepage
   explained as protocol://host name/ filename

2. (a) WAN typically uses external communications cabling (eg BT); LAN uses own internal cabling
   WAN has lower data transfer rate than LAN
   WAN has higher level of data corruption
   (b) **technical**
   communication between computers—need modems, WAN access software;
   maintenance (was one of the 4 the expert in solving technical problems)—use e-mail to communicate
   social
   less interaction—set-up video (or at least e-mail) conferencing

2. (continued)

(c) (i) web browser

(ii) use search engine with complex query
gnu or wildebeest and photo
look at websites, find a suitable one, download picture

(iii) picture may be copyright—if so permission must be obtained

3.
(a) (i) **peer-peer**—no one fileserver, computers share access to hard discs and peripherals

client-server—one computer acts as file server

(ii) only 3 computers, so network traffic relatively light
difficult to justify cost of an extra computer to act as fileserver

(iii) eg Windows 95, Windows 2000, MacOS . . .

(b) (i) *Two of* UTP cable, fibre optic cable, co-axial cable
UTP is cheap, or fibre optic high bandwidth

(ii) 10 or 100 Megabits per second

(iii) **CS** = carrier sense = only transmits when no network traffic

MA = multiple access = any station can access at any time

CD = collision detect = all transmitting stations stop transmitting if multiple signals detected

4.
(a) (i) a network of networks

(ii) *any 2 from* improved communications software-/-reduced access costs-/-improved modem speeds-/-higher computer ownership

(b) (i) Transmission Control Protocol/Internet Protocol

(ii) data to be transmitted is broken up into smaller packets, with address information which can be routed independently across the network(s)

(iii) **IP** layer concerned with ensuring that data packets find their way across network to correct machine

TCP layer concerned with control of data flow, with ensuring delivery of data (in correct order)

(c) (i) Transport layer

(ii) Network layer

Section III—Multimedia Technology

1. (a) Names or description of icon based and script based

Advantages: *for each type, any one of*

icon based—sophisticated applications can be built without scripting; offers icons, pull down menus; better for beginners; drag and drop facilities

script based—scripting computer programs may be defined to carry out the interaction; precise timing of events can be obtained

Disadvantages: *for each type, any one of*

icon based—slightly less accurate timings and less control over interactivity than scripting

scripting—may be more difficult to assemble multimedia elements by scripting, novice users may find difficulty creating overall flow of the presentation

(b) (i) *One of* reduces time taken to transfer data—less storage

(ii) eg MPEG layer 3 (MP3) *two points from* "perceptual noise shaping"-/-analyses sound to eliminate "unheard" element-/-sampled at 32 to 48 kHz-/-a lossy compression method

(c) **JPEG**—large number of colours (millions), recognised by a large no of applications

GIF —bitmap; allows transparent background, limited to 256 colours
—includes data compression, which increases its effectiveness, especially with scanned photos
—compression allows it to be transferred quickly across the Internet, and it also supports a variety of colours and various resolutions. It can also be viewed by people using any browser

TIFF—bitmap
—can support any size, resolution, colour and depth
—supported by many applications
—can be black and white, gray-scaled, or colour which allows for a very versatile usage. TIFF files are also portable because they are supported by both Mac and PC applications. TIFFs print slowly and resizing TIFFs can distort the image. Not all applications can read compressed files. Does not support vector graphics

Computing Higher
2000 (contd.)

1. (c) (continued)
    BMP—bitmap; windows paint files; images using 1, 4 or 8 bit per pixel must have a colour map (2, 16 or 256 respectively)
    — standard usage in all the Windows applications
    — device independent which means that the bitmap specifies pixel colour in a form independent of the method used by a display to represent colour
    — requires lots of memory as each pixel must be stored individually

    PICT—vector and bitmap;
    — supported by all graphics packages that run on Macintosh computers
    — original version supported only 8 colours but new versions including PICT2 support 32-bit colour (millions of colours)

    EPS —(encapsulated PostScript)
    — usually bit-mapped
    — for display purposes
    — supported by any application that uses the PostScript language ie Adobe
    — the graphics file format that is used by the PostScript language. Can be either binary or ASCII.
    — unlike PostScript it includes a bit-mapped representation of the graphic for display, while PostScript contains only the commands for printing the graphic
    — EPS files are larger than comparable TIFFs. EPS files can be written as either binary code or ASCII test. ASCII EPS is easier to transfer to another computer platform. Binary EPS is up to 50% smaller and prints faster. However, some printers and software can't handle the binary format

2. (a) **OCR operates by**
    — OCR (Pattern matching) software matches element of bit mapped graphic to known characters and produces a text file (WP document) based on the character matches

   (b) Two comparisons based on:
    DTP
    — sophisticated integration of text and graphics
    — more powerful editing features
    — freely manipulated on page layout
    — may be able to transfer directly into HTML format
    — text and static graphics only

    Hypermedia
    — able to link video and sound elements
    — more memory hungry
    — flexible, interactive

   (c) Brief description of any three from: skewing; distorting; perspective; blending; smearing; cropping; panning

   (d) linked elements through which the user can navigate WP—data is static

3. (a) *(candidates may answer in terms of the function of **three separate boards** (see below) or in terms of **one board** which replaces all three boards eg MICROMOTION DC30 which can capture full screen video at up to 30 frames per second, compress data using motion JPEG to 3% of its original size and output to monitor, TV or video cassette)*
    — video capture board takes analogue image and converts it to digital signal that the computer can process
    — no of frames per second depends on size of image being captured, the colour depth and quality of capture board
    (accept answers which relate to actual makes of video capture board)
    — video compression board
      MPEG technology compresses data to 2% of its size without loss of quality
    — video playback board
      takes over this task from CPU, which can carry on other tasks whilst the video playback board processes data and displays it on the monitor

   (b) **user/presentation level**
    — presentation software: authoring packages/presentation packages which handle animations, video and audio
    — flexible HCI; navigation tools (candidates may answer in terms of actual packages such as Macromedia Director, Hyperstudio, Illuminatis)
    — hyperlinking
    — software allows alteration of frame rate, colour depth, cut and paste

    operating system
    — forms bridge between user and hardware
    — provides special commands to control CD-ROM players, play sound files etc (icon based selection of operations at this level eg play, rewind, record etc)
    *(—the software component that enables communication with a device. In most cases, the driver also manipulates the hardware in order to transmit the data to the device. However, device drivers associated with programs typically perform only the **data translation**; these higher-level drivers then rely on lower-level drivers to actually **send** the data to the device. Many devices, such as video adapters, do not work properly (or at all) without the correct device drivers installed on the computer.)*

3. (b) (continued)
   low-level software (device drivers)
   — special commands to **send** data to devices eg CD-ROM players
   — the device driver is designed specifically for both the hardware and the operating system (platform specific)
   hardware devices
   — sound card; speakers; analogue interface; digital interface

   (c) *any two valid points eg*
   — people shouldn't copy other peoples' designs and claim them as their own (effectively robbing the true authors of their recognition and possible income)
   — individuals should copyright their work which gives them legal rights to prevent this from happening (legal action can be taken against the plagiariser)
   — authorisation needs to be obtained to use others' work and the source should be acknowledged

4. (a) pitch; length; attack; delay; volume; (accept answers which are less technically well defined such as: which note, how long, how loud, how high, how low)

   (b) (i) sequenced more flexible because *(two brief points from)*
       — data is more flexible because discrete note can be changed (number — musical equivalent of a WP package. MIDI tracks can be created, edited and combined to form a score; score is built up of a series of channels
       — no background noise to eliminate
       (ii) *any two from* alter instrument; alter pitch/length of note; copy and paste track

   (c) **Frequency Modulation** *any two from*
       — combines several simple waveforms to produce a complex waveform
       — the wider the range, the more realistic the sound
       Wavetable Synthesis *any two from*
       — sound samples are taken and digitally manipulated to produce different tones
       — quality depends on sampling frequency
       — software controlled method of generating sound

Computing Higher 2001

Section I

1. (a) Bus **or** Ring **or** Star (**NOT** Mesh)
   (Have to accept tree—"star of stars")
   + Appropriate diagram with at least **one** relevant labels
   Amendment—no half marks

   (b) Network card **or** NIC **or** networking card **or** Ethernet card (etc)

2. (a) When the processor is servicing a peripheral a buffer temporarily stores the data being sent in RAM (thus freeing the processor to carry out other tasks)

   (b) When printer is accessed over a network **or** When large files have to be dealt with **or** When advanced management of printing jobs has to be exercised (ordering, costing etc)

3. Description based on:
   editing (moving, resizing etc) eg can you select a part of the graphic by clicking on it; if so, vector
   Amount of storage required
   Resolution dependancy eg if it becomes "blocky", when enlarged then bit-mapped
   Quality of print outs

4. (a)
   $3 \times 4 \times 600 \times 600 \times 8 = 34\,560\,000$ bits
   $34\,560\,000/(8 \times 1024 \times 1024) = 4\cdot12$ Mb **or**
   $3 \times 4 \times 600 \times 600$ pixels = $4\,320\,000$ pixels
   256 colours $\Rightarrow$ 1 byte per pixel $\Rightarrow$ $4\,320\,000$ bytes
   so $4\,320\,000/1024/1024$ Mb = $4\cdot1$ Mb

   (b) Zip drive **or** Jazz drive **or** Hard Disc drive **or** DAT drive **or** CD-R drive *(not CD-ROM)* **or** DVD-R drive
   All of the above have enough storage capacity to store the file ie has more than $4\cdot1$ Mb capacity

5. (a) -128 to 127—*no alternative values, but allow -2^7 etc*

   (b) (i) Mantissa—precision is increased *(allow accuracy)*
       (ii) Exponent—range of numbers is increased

6. Components with two stable states are used to represent 0's and 1's

7. Each memory location is identified by a unique address.

8. (a) Counting Occurrences **or** (iii) **or** 3

   (b) User Guide
   Technical Guide

   (c) If changes have to be made to the guides then it is simpler to send out a new CD
   Also cheaper than printing out hard copies of new guides

9. (a) Analysis—understanding of client's problem into a precise specification, clarifying the requirements
   Design—planning of solution to problem, outlining the solution

   (b) The action of going back through a stage and rethinking, redoing
   A stage is revisited following testing or other further stage of refinement

Computing Higher 2001 (cont.)

10. (a) To allow other programmers to understand the code; In case changes have to be made later

    (b) Any **two** of the following:
    Modular code
    Internal commentary
    Indentation (accept structured listing)
    Meaningful variable and subprogram names/identifiers

11. (i) editor—to enable creation of program source code, enter and make changes to code

    (ii) translator—to allow the program to run, convert HLL code into machine code

    (iii) error tracing tool—to enable the searching for logic errors throughout the code during controlled execution to help identify the location of errors
    Must make clear that error tracing is not about syntax errors

12. (a) (i) Local variable—variable used exclusively within subprogram, scope limited to a single subprogram

    (ii) Subprograms can be run separately from rest of code, if use local variables subprogram can only affect the value of a variable within the subprogram—all data transfer between subprograms must be made explicit using parameter passing

    (b) array
    data structure eg linked list etc

Section II

13. (a) (i) Status information: Device selection
    Speed Conversion—to compensate for differences between processor and peripheral in terms of speed (ie buffering, latching);
    Data representation—to convert analogue to digital, serial to parallel (accept voltage)

    (ii) To allow the connection of any peripheral to the computer
    Many different peripherals on the market, too complex if each one had a different interface
    So that no incompatibility problems arise between the peripheral and computer. To allow peripherals by different manufacturers to be compatible with most cpus

    (iii) Driver, hardware driver

    (b) Difficult to compare different manufacturers as:
    The actual process being carried out by a single instruction may be very different
    Don't know how many instructions per second can be processed
    The "speed" of the computer may depend on other factors such as internal bus widths, type of processor,
    Speed of peripherals/interfaces USB etc
    Use of cache (Level 2, Level 1)
    Speed of memory bus (PC100, PC133 etc)
    Different length of time to execute instruction

    (c) Address bus must be 24 bits
    Each location is 4 bytes long. $64/4 = 16$ so need $16 \times 1024 \times 1024$ locations (ie addresses) ie $2^4 \times 2^{10} \times 2^{10} = 2^{24}$ addresses
    No of addresses = $2^{\text{address bus width}}$
    So address bus width is 24 bits

    (d) Register with Data Protection Registrar
    Keep data safe and secure
    Update data regularly
    Allow inspection of data by data subject
    Correct errors in data if demonstrated
    Adhere to registered disclosure protocol

14. (a) 1 User has to type from keyboard (not particularly easy for some), validity errors very likely
    Endless possible entries could be given which the program would have to check

    2 Set number of entries chosen from menu, validity errors impossible
    Good control of mouse required to select country, difficult for user to see all at once

    3 Quickest method for user as typing in one character will restrict choices on screen
    Set number of entries chosen from menu, validity errors possible but unlikely
    Keyboard and/or mouse could be used

    (b) Who will the typical users be?
    level of knowledge of users? (will they be able to spell correctly?)
    Is it comprehensive enough for end user?
    Is speed of data entry an issue?

    (c) Use range of test cases with suitable users
    Experiment with typical end user ie have the program tested by **many** potential users;
    test with a range of user **types**

    (d) • Array of names stored for validation would need changed for all 3
    • Menu choices changed for 2 and 3. 1 requires no change
    • 2 requires editing of the list (probably a data file)
    • 3 may also require some coding, although the algorithm for scrolling the list automatically should be generic, suitable for any country's name

15. (a) Video card—to input video frames
Large RAM—to view video on screen
Large backing storage—to allow editing of large video data files
High resolution, colour, high refresh rate monitor—for detailed editing work

(b) (i) Digital or optical zoom, LCD screen, resolution, colour depth, capacity
Accept also lens, media card requirements, bundled software

(ii) No need to develop film or to buy film—so reduced time
No wastage of film if wrong shot taken, able to delete unwanted photos; data can be downloaded directly to computer for editing and storage; immediate hard copy possible

(c) • high resolution (over 600dpi) to give non-grainy images;
• must be colour rather than black/white
• "photo quality" ie larger number of inks, variable dot size etc

(d) database software (or searchable web pages) to store images
in structured way with keywords etc for searching
graphics storage requirements are likely to be high
so this would probably need to be held on a CD, so a CD-writer would be required
Alternatively
hierarchical folder structure with descriptive folder and file names
AND thumbnails of photographs as icons, etc

16. (a) *Two points along the lines of*:
The ability to attach code to an event such as a mouse click or a window opening.
Allows ease of interface design incorporating text, data entry boxes, buttons . . . ;
The availability of pre-written code to generate dialog boxes, buttons etc
non-linear program structure allows program responds to events dictated by the user

(b) *Two points along the lines of*:
Programs written in procedural language have definite start/end points.
Order of execution determined by algorithm rather than events.
Fixed algorithm for execution of program, rather than depending on user.

(c) *Two brief descriptions of relevant functions such as*:
In file management system—loading or saving of data file
In input/Output system—mouse clicks, keystrokes buffered until application needs them
In memory management—allocate memory for data

(d) *Two points made from each of Advantages and Difficulties, such as*:
Advantages—no need for specialist programming knowledge as macros may be used to "program" applications; Speed of development, as much of the functionality is already present within the application; data structures already exist; algorithms for searches and comparisons already exist
Difficulties—may be a lack of necessary functions within application eg storage and updating of totals might require global variables; Lack of flexibility in design of screen display—may be restricted by application may required coding in a scripting language (eg VBA); means user must have the appropriate application package

17. (a) IF mark >=0 AND mark <=100

(b) *Two points from*:
makes program more modular;
allows same variable names (eg loop counters) in more than one subprogram;
makes data flow explicit improving readability and therefore maintainability;
accept description of portability

(c) (i) no significant difference
(ii) 1-D array better, as makes clear the fact that the 10 marks are all related
(iii) much simpler to pass a single array than ten separate variables

(d) By Reference passes pointer rather than whole data structure
By Reference allows parameter to be altered in the procedure, whereas by value any changes within procedure are not passed out of the procedure

18. (a) List could be passed by value but most languages require arrays to be passed by reference.
Could also have a parameter called "found" type boolean (or integer) passed by value

(b) (position < size of list) AND (item not found) AND (still items in list to search)

(c) *Any two of*
smaller source code size
improved reliability since code already tested
reduced requirement for maintenance
debugging is simplified

(d) (i) removal of the condition "item not found"
(ii) require an array of data type integer to store list of positions
require a count of type integer to store number of items found

Computing Higher
2001 (cont.)

Section III
Part A—Artificial Intelligence

19. (a) (i) analysis and design
    (ii) knowledge engineer extracts specialist knowledge from domain expert during analysis;
    the design stage is done by the knowledge engineer with no input needed from domain expert

    (b) (i) expert system = user interface + inference engine + knowledge base
    expert system shell = user interface + inference engine (but no knowledge base)
    (ii) no need to code user interface and inference engine; but may be less flexible

    (c) (i) ADVISE wind speed increase (0·9) IF direction = S AND pressure falling
    ADVISE wind speed increase (0·5) IF direction = N AND pressure falling
    (ii) certainty factor (eg 0·9 for very likely, 0·5 for may) indicate the level of confidence in the advice
    for certainty factor on its own
    (iii) response should describe issue of legal accountability for information used

20. (a) (i) `X = scotland, Y = 4406`
    (ii) `?mountain(X,scotland,_)`
    [could have a variable instead of _]

    (b) match clause 6; instantiate X to ben-nevis; first sub-goal
    `mountain(ben_nevis,scotland,H);`
    match at clause 3; instantiate H=4406;
    2nd sub-goal 4406>3000 is TRUE, so `munro(ben_nevis)` is TRUE

    (c) `furth(X) if mountain(X,Y,Z) and Z>3000 and not Y=scotland`

    (d) (i) `munro(X) if height(X,H) and country(X,scotland) and H>3000`
    (ii) search time will be longer due to the greater number of clauses

21. (a) finding a representation for the current state of the game (positions of pieces); there are many rules to be coded; the number of positions multiplies very quickly and unmanageably when looking ahead; the need for a function which can evaluate possible positions

    (b) need not just the development but also the impact
    hugely increased processor speeds allow large numbers of positions to be evaluated in a reasonably short time
    huge increases in memory allow many possible game positions to be stored simultaneously
    parallel processing allows subdivision of the search task

    (c) heuristics allow a smaller number of probably better moves to be selected from the large number of possible moves, thus speeding up the process of determining the next move

    (d) ability to learn from successes and failures, so that performance improved over time

    (e) (i) any description related to machine learning, creativity, natural language processing, pattern recognition (context) "justified" reasoning. Vision systems
    (ii) either an area of human ability must be described with a reason why technology could never out-perform a human (may be a technical or philosophical reason) or a reasoned argument that the brain is simply a machine, which, given sufficient research can be modelled in software or hardware

22. (a) (i) smaller number of neurons/perceptrons in artificial network
    (ii) given stimuli; "trainer" gives feedback on whether or not output was "correct"; an algorithm adjusts the weights linking the perceptrons; process repeated many times until the output is reliably correct
    (iii) any reasonable example eg financial modelling, handwriting recognition
    (iv) there is no algorithm, so it cannot be stated with complete certainty that the correct response will always be given (just like a human expert)

    (b) (i) increased processor speed allows large amounts of data to be processed in real-time; increases in memory allow pattern-matching to be developed with large graphical data
    (ii) they can "see" and therefore identify the object on which they are working; they are less likely to damage other machines or humans if they can "see" them
    (iii) ability to learn (eg a welding robot might be able to develop its own set of moves in an industrial process)

Section III
Part B—Computer Networking

23. (a) modem, communications software
    modem—convert digital signals to analogue suitable for telecoms
    software—control the modem, encode data, manage flow of data between laptop and remote server

    (b) (i) laptop computer and remote server must be using same standards for sending and receiving data
    (ii) communication speed, size of data packet, start and stop bits

Official SQA Answers to Higher Computing

23. **(continued)**
    (c) (i) Competition between newspapers for exclusive stories.
        (ii) Descriptions of data encryption, login with passwords, also "use of virtual private networks".
    (d) *Descriptions of two of*:
        Higher speed of transfer;
        Lower error rate;
        different protocols in use

24. (a) (i) Router; accept gateway but not a bridge!!
        (ii) Internetwork; accept WAN
             Note NOT intranet
    (b) TCP responsible for breaking file data into packets, verifying delivery, reassembling packets
        IP responsible for delivery to correct network address, including routing if necessary
    (c) Leased line has higher bandwidth than ISDN but more expensive to lease. ISDN line rental less but call charges apply whenever it is used.
        Leased line permanently available. ISDN would require one side "dial up" the other when communication has to take place.
    (d) (i) could be http or ftp
        (ii) **Advantages**
            A single server would be easier to manage—software and data only have to be loaded to one site. Data is more likely to be up to date and accurate if there is only one copy in use at any one time.
            Disadvantages
            Security of information, need a backup. Information not always available as server may have to be taken off line for servicing or updating of information. 3 clear points from either advantage/disadvantage
            If cost mentioned, there must be reference to balance between capital and bandwidth

25. (a) (i) peer to peer network
        (ii) Allow access only to named users—do not allow "guest" access.
        (iii) Set access rights of shared folder to read only.
    (b) (i) client-server network
        (ii) server computer
             server software at server, client software at each station

    (c) (i) **data security**—all shared files on a single server which can be protected from unauthorised access by password or physically locking it away in a secure room. Users can be set up and access rights controlled centrally
        data integrity—all shared data accessed from single server. Only one copy being used by all users therefore more likely to be correct and accurate
        (ii) E-mail
             Need a server to store mail for each mail user.

26. (a) Set parameters for communication—speed etc
        Implement IP over telephone line (SLIP, PPP)
    (b) Use search engine
        Search for design notation **AND** software development (*Note must be complex search*)
    (c) A—protocol, B—host name, C—file name/path to file
    (d) The school may have a faster link—possible ISDN–to ISP
        Gateway (proxy server) may cache files locally
        Schools computers may render pages faster, giving appearance of faster downloads
    (e) (i) Downloading of files may introduce virus to school network
            To prevent breaches of copyright
            Excessive use of bandwidth
        (ii) Firewall

Section III
Part C—Computer Programming

27. (a) 2D array with 2 columns and 5 rows (in this example)
        each row of the array holds the division result and the remainder
        Could also be a 2D array with 5 columns and 2 rows where each column holds the division result and remainder
    (b) The algorithm below is one possible answer. There may be other possible answers
        iterate = 0 (lower array bound);
            while (decConvert <> 0)
                begin
                    remainder = decConvert MOD 2
                    decConvert = decConvert DIV 2;
                    array[1][iterate] = decConvert;
                    array[2][iterate] = remainder;
                    add 1 to iterate
            end while
        Key points—management of array pointer, allocation of values to array
        Range of values which can be dealt with limited by size of array.

Computing Higher 2001 (contd.)

27. (continued)

(c) (i) Either of the following descriptions

1. The array could be subdivided and values of the division held in one half which the remainders are held in the other. A fixed offset value would provide a paired matching.

   OR

2. The two values could be held in adjacent array positions with each value pair offset in the array by adding 2 to the index position of the first pair value.
   It would also be possible to use a 1D array of records

(ii) Any **TWO** of the following:
- the code to create the array and to traverse it would be more complex
- complexity leads to likelihood of more errors
- complexity makes it more difficult to debug
- complexity increases time required to maintain the code

28. (a) (i) ONE of: end of file, array bounds error, insufficient file access privileges, file does not exist
Not Div by zero!

(ii) Variety of possibilities depending upon implementation. Must relate to error mentioned in (i)
eg use conditional loop to control reading from file,—so that end of array is detected.
test for end of file or array full conditions—so that reading is stopped (detect return code on attempt to open—report this).
detect error as an exception/through error trapping routine—report error.

(b) set position_array to 1;
loop while NOT EOF(textfile)
   begin
      read name and store in array1[position_array]
      read name and store mark in array2[position_array]
      increment position_array
   end loop

(c) (i) care has to be taken to sort corresponding values in both arrays

(ii) Would only require one array data structure. Clearer program task.

(d) (i) TWO of: that the array is not full already; the "top" of the existing data has not been reached; whether the new name is later in alphabetical order than the current item

(ii) Suitable diagram showing "bubbling" up of array elements "above" the insertion point

29. (a)

3	← Top
7	

(b) upper limit = 3

(c) if stack pointer ◇ upper limit then
   begin
      stack pointer = stack pointer + 1
      stack[stack pointer] = symbol
   end

(d) (i) stack overflow

(ii) by first checking that the stack pointer ◇ upper array bounds

(iii) the program could trap the error using the test given in (ii)
the program could report a stack overflow error

30. (a) *In these responses, head refers the point in the queue which will be processed next, tail to the last item entered into the queue. The queue is assumed to fill from the lower bound to the upper bound of the array. A basic queue implementation is assumed.*

(i) pointers to head and tail of queue (both required)

(ii) head pointer is 1 less than lower bound of array. Tail pointer is upper bound of array

(b) (i) Problem—due to upper bound condition—even when items dequeued, no way to add item to queue.

(ii) Either move items down in array, adjusting pointers OR implement circular queue, with modulo arithmetic to wrap round pointer values OR implement queue using eg linked list

(c) suitably labelled diagram showing the tail pointer being incremented and the head remaining static

(d) set pointer to head of queue
loop while pointer ◇ queue tail
   begin
      if username of queue[pointer] = searchitem then
         increment occurences
      increment pointer
   end loop

Section III
Part D—Multimedia Technology

31. (a) (i) an authoring tool is a program which helps you write hypertext or multimedia applications through the creation and manipulation of multimedia elements into a single presentation

(ii) *any two from*:
— links objects such as text, illustrations, sound;
— defines objects relationships to one another and sequences them in appropriate order;
— may support a scripting language for more sophisticated applications;
— buttons to control the flow of information, allow choices to be made, to initiate events
— menu selections to allow choice
— events which are inactive until the user initiates them
— navigation maps which allows different routes to different sources of information

(b) *Two points for each item, for example*
optical data storage—description of developments eg speed of disks and drives; CD-ROM to DVD allowing larger storage of data, hence allowing all elements of multimedia to be stored. Faster transfer of data.
sound card technologies—description of sound card developments eg development from single bleep sounds to 8 bit cards; stereo; CD quality 16 bit audio; wavetable sound; storing the waveform "signatures" of real musical instruments in the sound card's memory, then playing them back at varying pitch in order to reproduce different notes; current sound cards provide a MIDI interface (standard hardware and software protocol for allowing musical instruments to communicate with each other); many sound cards provide FM synthesis for backward compatibility with older cards and software.
Sound cards commonly use 8 or 16 bit samples at sampling rates from about 4000 to 44,000 samples per second.
The samples may also be contain one channel (mono) or two (stereo).
Most sound cards provide the capability of mixing, combining signals from different input sources; no longer dependent upon internal speakers. High quality stereo sound, playback of audio CDs and digitised sounds. Digital in/out capability therefore no loss in A to D conversion

31. (continued)

(c) *accept any* **one** *description from*:
MIDI (.mid)—MIDI stands for Music Instruments Digital Interface; a standard for transmitting musical information between electronic instruments and computers; size of a MIDI file is small; quality of the music is very good
WAVE (.wav)—WAVE files are sound data-digital representation of an analog signal; linearly encoded; files can be large; can be stereo/mono 8/16 bit
UNLAW (.au)—the original NeXt machine sound standard. It is a digitised sound data file similar to WAVE files and takes a lot of storage space. Common on Unix/Sun platforms
MOD (.mod)—a collection of sample data and a description of how to play these samples in a certain order, pitch, and distortion on four channels; samples don't necessarily have to be from real musical instruments. The MOD format reveals a big advantage over the WAVE and MIDI formats. Any natural sound can be used as an instrument, where as MIDI can't do this. The size of a MOD file is much smaller compared to a WAVE file that produces the same sound.
AIFF (.aiff)—The Audio Interchange File Format allows one program open a digital recording created by another program. The format actually used on CDs—though it can represent the encoded digitised sound at different sample rates and
SND(.snd)—An Amiga sound extension that is a sound data file
MP3—supported by many software applications, can be used for DVD, portable music players, web music. Compression ratio of the order of 10:1 compared to eg AIFF

32. (a) *any* **three** *from*:
— hierarchical structure of pages; number of pages; interaction and links;
— storyboard showing flow of presentation;
— list of hardware, software and media elements used
— order of multimedia elements
— number of different elements?
— consistent user response structures (dialog boxes etc)
— consistent navigation prompts (bars, arrows etc)
— error reporting
— background

(b) — most authoring packages are icon based and developer may need to perform an action which is not available in the menus; more complex tasks and accurate timing sequences may be obtained
— scripts may be "saved" and used in other presentations ie reusable code

Computing Higher 2001 (contd.)

32. **(b)** **(continued)**
—script based allows more flexibility for developers; Icon based may not offer the necessary tools required

(c) (i) *Any **three** of*:
image size; colour depth; frame rate/refresh rate/scan rate; brightness; resolution; display mechanism

(ii) video adapter card contains the circuitry which generates the signals for the appropriate video display; contains a certain amount of RAM (VRAM—buffers image data); better quality and larger images can be obtained by increasing VRAM available
most cards support 3D, have a good refresh rate, 32 bit + colour depth, high resolution, motion compensation

33. **(a)** (i) *description of characteristics from* bit depth, colour, resolution
bit depth—scanner records varying amounts of information about each pixel (more pixels = better quality). The amount of information that the scanner can remember about each pixel is commonly referred to as bit depth. A bit depth of 12 can identify 4,096 grey scales.
Colour—how "true to life" the digitised colours are for quality photographs or other images required
Resolution—measures how many pixels a scanner can assign to any given image or document. Most scanners start at about 300 × 300 dots/pixels per inch –r reads 90,000 pixels per square inch for the image being scanned

(ii) **handheld:** dragging scan head over the image; useful for scanning objects other than flat pages; poorer quality than flat bed; but less expensive
flatbed: operates like a photocopier; scan head moves over image; can accommodate paper sizes larger than A4 and large books and magazines
sheet fed: limited to A4 sheets; image is fed by mechanical rollers and scanned one line at a time until complete image has been processed
Characteristics in terms of
High resolution for graphic capture (OCR software—for text capture)
At least 36 bit colour depth—for photographs

(b) Answers **must** include descriptions. Other graphics formats are possible—
TIFF—is compressed format, therefore more economical in storage space; a common graphics format which is easily imported into WP and DTP packages; TIFF can handle monochrome, greyscale, 8 bit or 24 bit colour images
GIF—only allows 256 colours
JPEG—lossy compression (*allow detail loss*)
EPS—needs Postscript printer
BMP—less flexible

(c) *Really looking for the "advanced" image processing tasks as listed in the Arrangements with brief descriptions.*
*Therefore **three** of*:
Rotating, flipping, resizing, scaling, cropping, filling, morphing, Gamma correction image contrasting, outline sharpening
With description of the task carried out.

(d) Response should be a comparison, eg
ASCII—text will easily transfer to any application; however
RTF—will retain formatting features

34. **(a)** (i) description of MPEG/JPEG; lossy compression; eg compression of graphical data using MPEG where only the changes from one frame to another are stored instead of the entire frame
OR description of RLE, Huffman or other "standard" data compression technique
ADPCM—Audio, only stores deltas so only 1/4 of storage required
AC-3—Audio, noise reduction used
MPEG—Video, only saves deltas between successive frames

(ii) any suitable description eg lossy compression technique for graphic or sound files; any situation where removal of some data would be acceptable and loss is not noticeable to the human ear and eye
non lossy for text data where loss of any data would be unacceptable

(b) *Description of any **two** from*:
Vector: WMF, PICT, EPS, CDR
Bitmapped: BMP, TIFF, GIF, PCX, JPEG
(+ any other acceptable answers)
with some description of characteristics of each named filetype eg
GIF—bitmapped, lossless compression, only 256 colours
BMP—bitmapped, Windows standard, large files
TIFF—bitmapped, mostly used for DTP, variable storage structure
JPEG—bitmapped, lossy compression, most commonly used format
CDR—vector, proprietary, used for Corel Graphics
EPS—vector, encapsulated postscript

34. (continued)

(c) *Any **three** from*:
Blend—sharp edges on images blend into one another (colour graduations)
Smear—softens an image by smudging/smearing darker areas of the image
Colour depth—increasing the colour depth retains all the image's colours, decreasing the colour depth may reduce the number of colours below that currently used by the image. Low colour depths = smaller file sizes
Colour palette—converts the logical colour numbers stored in each pixel of video memory into physical colours that can be displayed on the monitor. Changes to the palette affect the whole screen at once and can be used to produce special effects which would be much slower to produce by updating pixels. **Also allow** Scaling, resizing, filling, cropping, pixel editing, airbrush red-eye correction

Computing Higher 2002

Section I

1. (a) Fewer rules of arithmetic to be encoded in circuitry
Less chance of signal degradation changing data
Binary numbers easily represented using digital electronic devices
Due to 2 states (1 and 0) this can easily be represented as 0 volts and some volts electronically

   (b) 11110010 or (ii)

2. (a) Each character is represented by a 7 bit **binary** number (accept 8 bit or 1 byte)

   (b) The complete list of all characters which a device **or the system** can handle

3. The instructions which control the processor are stored in memory along with the data which is to be processed—separate from the processing unit
This means that the same processing unit can be used for many different tasks. Just change the program

4. (i) Software which controls and maintains the computer system

   (ii) Programs which **provide tools and functions** to enable the computer to carry out specific tasks for the user. eg wp, db etc

5. (a) (i) Processor speed, RAM. Backing Storage, Number of processors

   (ii) Server should have faster processor, more RAM, more backing storage space

5.(continued)

(b) Creating packets to be placed on the network, checking the address of incoming packets, encryption, Data Integrity, multi user access (user login, checking passwords, creating users and groups etc) *Any **one***

6. To store data in transit between cpu and device to make up for difference in speed,
To perform data conversion (eg difference in voltage, difference in data representation),
Control signals, Provide status information,
Recognition of device information

7. (a) *Any suitable response of the following type*
   - To fully explain the needs of the client
   - To fully specify the problem
   - To produce and agree a problem specification
   - To observe, clarify and model the current system

   (b) Requirements specification, operational requirements specification or problem specification

   (c) **Corrective** maintenance is the changing of code to fix errors found after release of the software
   Adaptive maintenance is the amending of the program to cope with its new environment, (to remove clashes with other programs or to optimise for the OS)
   Perfective maintenance is the amending of the code to include new features and optimisations suggested by the users after release

8. (a) A module library contains a number of pre-written routines which the programmer can use within a program

   (b) ***Two*** *of the following responses*
   - Use of parameters
   - No global variables
   - Self-contained
   - Good documentation
   Any other valid

   (c) Robust software does not crash if invalid data is entered
   Software is fit for purpose if it matches the specification arrived at during the analysis phase in consultation with the client. It does the task as specified

9. Linear search

10. Features could be indentation of sub-clauses, blank lines between code blocks, capitalised/bold/colour keywords, line numbers

Computing Higher
2002 (contd.)

11. A clear description of the passing of the value of the variable into a module, where any changes do not affect the original value afterwards eg a second copy of variable is created to be used within the module, thus unaffecting the original

12. Syntax error is a grammar error eg PINT "Hello world!"
    This is introduced at implementation
    A logic error is introduced at the analysis or design phase and affects the algorithm eg LET months = years * 10

Section II

13. (a) **ALU**—carries out arithmetic and logical operations
    Control Unit—manages fetching, decoding and executing of instructions
    Registers—temporary storage areas

    (b) Set up address on address bus and open memory location
    Read line on control bus activated
    Data bus carries data from memory location to processor

    (c) Faster processors to enable instructions to be carried out quicker. Larger RAM to enable larger programs and data to be loaded at the same time. Wider data buses. Faster clock speeds. Caches.
    (Although Parallel processing, RISC and pipelining are not explicit in the arrangements, they could be possible responses)

    (d) 2^{24} memory locations and 16 bits for each storage location
    16777216×16 bits = 33554432 bytes = 32 Mb

14. (a) **Pseudocode**—step by step algorithm written in English or
    Flow chart—graphical breakdown of steps required

    (b) **Editor**—to create and amend the code—Implementation/testing/maintenance
    Interpreter/compiler—to translate HLL into machine code Implementation/testing/maintenance
    Debugger/error tracing—to find and identify errors—Implementation/testing/maintenance

    (c) Data types and structures required, operations required
    User interface required, type of task (arithmetic, problem solving etc), what hardware is needed to support the program, typical end users, what environment will the program operate, the type of problem to be solved AND exemplification

    (d) Modular code, meaningful variable/procedural names, internal commentary, indentation

    (e) **Normal**—1·5, 2, 3 etc to test that the program works correctly (reliable and correct)
    Boundary—0, 40 or 60 or 100 or 24×7 to test extremes
    Exceptions—negative numbers, text to test that the program is robust and will not crash due to unexpected data

15. (a) **WP**—to produce and edit text for the newsletter
    Graphics—to edit pictures for the newsletter
    DTP—to produce newsletter page layouts
    DB—to maintain a database of members
    SS—to keep club accounts
    E-Mail client—to distribute newsletter electronically

    (b) Club members may have different hardware and/or software from club
    Use of standard data formats will enable transfer data between different platforms

    (c) description of a validation check on any field in the database
    could describe setting upper and lower limits when defining field or defining field as a list or drop down menu

    (d) recommend **either**, with any of the following advantages:
    digital camera: pictures available immediately; direct production of digital image; no need to buy film or a separate camera
    OR
    scanner: cheaper than a digital camera; can scan existing photographs; can be used for other purposes eg OCR

    (e) (i) a language which can be used to write programs (scripts) which control other applications or programs or are contained within an application

    (ii) could be used to write a macro (or script) to automate some process (eg a complex search/sort/layout process in the database)

16. (a) file management, memory management, input/output, HCI, command interpretation, program scheduling
    (allow any reasonable sub-functions of the above or descriptions of the above functions)

    (b) any **two** utilities eg virus checker, defragmenter, backup utility, sector editor, file repair utility

16. (continued)

(c) (i) eg optical disc, DAT, zip drive, jaz drive

(ii) eg
optical disc—allows files larger than 1·4 Mb to be saved on a portable device
DAT—allows fast backups to be made of the HD

(d) (Prolog or lisp)—program consists of facts and rules rather than a coded algorithm

(e) interpreter used during development as it allows easier editing and partial testing, errors more easily traced
compiler used to produce runnable machine code final version, faster execution

17. (a) Improves readability, aids maintenance, splits up problem into manageable sections, can allocate modules to members of team

(b) Makes the procedure more flexible, or re-usable

(c) (i) Less memory used to store integers, arithmetic more accurate, integers can be processed faster

(ii) Array of integers

(d) eg
If grade > = upper_grade AND grade < = lower_grade

(e) A conditional loop eg REPEAT or WHILE
loop until grade = sentinel_value
 get grade
  if grade not sentinal_value then
   process grade
  end if
 end of loop   or similar

18. (a) Consistency of input screens, use of on-line help, meaningful error messages, other valid answers

(b) **Position of maximum**—integer passed by reference
accident array—array of integer passed by reference

(c) A loop variable. Prevents the possibility of accidentally changing another variable with same name in other part of program. Local variable could also be used to store maximum value—*other answers are possible*

(d) (i) fixed loop, if structure

(ii) loop for current_position = 1 to 6 (or number_of_areas)
  if number at current_position > number at position_of_current_maximum then
   set position_of_current_maximum to current_position
  end if
 end of loop
other answers possible

Section III
Part A—Artificial Intelligence

19. (a) (i) She is the Knowledge Engineer

(ii) Dr Ridge is not an expert in bats and has to work with Tony to make sure that the finished system has the correct information. Tony is not familiar with the construction of computer programs.

(b) **Knowledge Base**—The list of facts and rules comprising the total information known by the system
Inference Engine—The mechanism by which the system chooses the fact or rule to apply to solve any given query. It employs pattern matching of the goals and sub-goals to the rules and facts in the knowledge base

(c) (i) **one**, or more, of the following points
• A list of sub-goals satisfied which has led to the response given
• A description of the reasons for the system suggesting this particular answer
• Explanation of **how** a solution was found or **why** a question is being asked

(ii) linking to the fact that BatSearch is a training program eg will help user to understand what the important factors are in identifying bats so that they can learn how to do this themselves

(iii) There is a legal requirement that bat handlers are licensed. If someone were trained by the expert system they might think that they had been given permission to handle bats. The law might consider the system to be partly responsible for this infringement

(d) Testing: to provide suitable test data. **Only domain experts has enough knowledge to test program**
Documentation: to check details of the information ie legal statement
Maintenance (Perfective)—any further developments volunteers need to know

20. (a) (i) "true" or "yes"

(ii) Goal **sentence**(badger meets otter) is matched at 10
Sub goal noun(badger) matched at 1
Sub goal verb(meets) matched at 6
Sub goal noun(otter) matched at 3
All three sub goals are true
Therefore goal is true

(b) (i) A = badger, C = fox

(ii) A clear description of the addition of a fourth sub-goal of the form **and not (A = C)**. (Allow various symbols for not equal to)

Computing Higher 2002 (contd.)

20. (continued)

(c)

Complex sentence(A B C D E)   if   adjective (A)
                          and noun(B)
                          and verb(C)
                          and adjective(D)
                          and noun(E)

(d) Answers should comment fully upon both of the following:
- Greatly increased number of **facts** for the system to deal with to represent all possible words
- Greater number of **rules** to express the variety of legal sentence structures

Alternative answers may comment upon the **technical** difficulties. These should make reference to the greatly increased memory/processor requirements

21. (a) Depth first follows one branch to its end before trying another branch.
Breadth first tests all nodes at one level before moving to next level.
use of memory to store previous successes is greater in breadth first, breadth first will find the best solution, depth first may go down a branch where there is no solution

(b) (i) This is a "rule of thumb" or supposition which directs the system towards where the solution is likely to be

(ii) The heuristic allows the size of the search space to be reduced. This will greatly decrease the time for finding the solution, as less of the tree will be traversed

(c) (i) response should make a clear connection between visual recognition systems and the manufacturing context eg
- Allows robots arms to check orientation of components
- Allows boards to be visually checked and rejected by system
- Reduction in the number of wasted components if checking done automatically at each stage

(ii) formal connection between the above points and a saving in time or cost eg less waste leads to reductions in costs—possible increase in profit

(d) **Procedural:**
Advantage—common language, many trained programmers, etc
Disadvantage—not so easy to model decision making process

Declarative:
Positive—suited to pattern matching/problem solving, uncertainty okay
Negative—requires specialist programmers

22. (a)
- these are numeric values of probability attached to facts
- they range between 0, for definitely false, and 1 for definitely true (or 0% to 100%)

(b) (i) A clear description of a diagnosis or process control application which includes **explicit** reference to certainty factors. **Must explain why advice is not definitive in this area**

(ii) Poor advice from system may lead to loss of money or physical harm to users (or users' clients). This may lead to legal action against developers. Users should be warned against using this advice exclusively. Disclaimers added to software

(c) This is a very wide area, which could include:
- Better storage media, which can store larger knowledge bases and access them faster
- Cheaper, faster RAM—more of the search tree held in memory, therefore "shortest path" optimisations can take place
- Digital optics—visual recognition systems etc
- Faster processors—larger throughput

(d) The ability to recognise (or identify) individual objects in a picture from a huge range of angles using colour, shading and prior experience
The ability to extrapolate 3D information from a 2D scene
Automatic adjustment to light
Depth perception
Concavity/convexity

(e)
- Inner layers of the net changing weighting values to reflect new knowledge
- Training and feedback changes weightings therefore improving knowledge

Section III
Part B—Computer Networking

23. (a) **Economic factor**—reduced comms costs/shared access to expensive equipment/geographic spread of organisations/competition/demand for up to date info
Technical factor—advances in computer technology **with exemplification**/new data transmission media and methods/international standards/improved software/Internet technology

23. (continued)

23. (b) (i) print server, communications server, applications server, e-mail server, proxy server, CD server

   (ii) print server—stores, and processes print jobs
   comms server—manages communications across the network
   e-mail server—holds mail prior to delivery (store and forward) etc

(c) It is client-server as a peer-peer network does not have dedicated servers

(d) user files are stored on the file server's HD
accept encryption if linked to **transmission** of data
user must log on using user ID and password
network OS checks this and only allows user to access appropriate files

(e) (i) all user files are stored centrally, and so copies need to be kept in case they are corrupted in any way

   (ii) suitable backing store (probably a tape drive), with automatic backup schedule (eg every 24 hours at midnight)

24. (a) (i) **repeater**—boosts signal where distance between nodes causes deterioration

   (ii) **bridge**—connects 2 networks using the same protocol

   (iii) **router**—connects networks in an internet work, sends packets of data towards the correct destination

(b) (i) **FTP**—allows files to be transferred between nodes on a network
   SMTP—controls the routing of e-mails across a network

   (ii) allows networks throughout the world of many types to communicate so long as they all use the same protocols

(c) www.billtheplumber.co.uk
+ more recognisable/memorable: clearly indicates a UK-based company
− cost of domain registration, lack of availability of domain name
www.freewebservices.com/users/pages/billtheplumber
+ probably free
− clumsy, difficult to remember name

(d) (i) eg internet allows "Bill" to advertise widely; on-line enquiries

   (ii) small company might not be able to afford to set up internet advertising, lack of expertise regular checking of feedback (e-mail) and/or web design (extra employee to pay perhaps?)

25. (a) shared access to printers
shared access to software/databases

(b) network interface card (eg ethernet card) to allow connection to network
network OS to allow communication with the network or NIC driver

(c) (i) easier to extend/alter or failure of 1 cable only affects one station

   (ii) a hub or switch to which all computers are connected at the centre of star

   (iii) 1 mark for **two** types—UTP (twisted pair, cat 5), Coax or fibre optic,
   UTP—Cheap, easy to install, fibre optic—higher bandwidth, less signal degradation Coax—cheap, reliable over short distances

(d) (i) an internetwork is 2 or more LANs connected to each other

   (ii) library users have access to software on school network
   school pupils have access to public library databases
   OR school pupils could access school network from library in the evening

26. (a) (i) LAN has higher bandwidth

   (ii) LAN mainly uses coaxial cable or UTP (fibre also possible)
   WAN uses trunk phone lines, satellite link, microwave link, fibre optic cable

(b) encryption of data; use of dedicated fibre optic cable
passwords not acceptable

(c) (i) 24 hour access using ATMs or Internet access or many different banks can be accessed other than one that holds account

   (ii) less need for manual counting/processing of money or paperwork

(d) (i) video conferencing or video phone

   (ii) need high speed modem, ISDN, cable modem, broadband or ADSL, webcam and video conferencing software

Section III
Part C—Computer Programming

27. (a) (i) The list must be sorted

   (ii) Binary search compares search item with item at middle of list in order to restrict further search. This only works if list is in order

(b) variable to store position of top of sub list, variable to store position of bottom of sub list, variable to store position of middle of sub list, variable to store search item
middle is calculated from top and bottom, search item is compared with item at middle of list

Computing Higher 2002 (contd.)

27. *(b)* (continued)

if search item is **smaller than the** item **at the middle of the** list then the contents of **top** variable are **set** to the **middle** variable −1

If greater than middle then bottom is set to middle +1

The middle is then re-calculated to start new search

(c) Binary Search : 2 Comparisons
Linear Search : 4 Comparisons

(d) When item to be searched for is first in list. Linear Search required 1 comparison— Binary Search requires 3 comparisons. Also short list as time is saved by not sorting

(e) A palmtop has limited storage and processing power

28. *(a)* (i) string array with 13 elements

(ii) Any **two** *of the following*:
more readable than 13 variables
ease of parameter passing
assists modularity
any other valid reason

(b) **Stack**—list/array where new items are pushed onto end of list and items popped from same end—operates under LIFO
Queue—list/array where items pushed onto end of list and items removed from head—operates under FIFO

(c)
- If card > 0 then   If there are any cards in the stack
- Let card$ = bank$(card)   record the top card
- Let card = card − 1   decrement the stack pointer

(d) Open (channel to) file
For member = 1 to 13 **or 1 to max**
    Write bank$(member) to file
End loop
Close (channel to) file

29. *(a)* any 2 from:
create file—to create a new file to receive the data
open file to write—to prepare the file to accept new data
append to file—to add a competitor's results to those already there
close file—to close the file when no further data is to be added
read from file—to retrieve the data for further processing

(b) record of:
name: string
bibno: integer
time: real
penalty: integer

(c) (i) any sort algorithm (likely answers will be selection, exchange (**bubble**), selection-exchange, quicksort)

(ii) accept answer as a description, a diagram showing an example list after each pass, or as pseudocode [*see www.cs.brockport.edu/cs/javasort.html for examples of algorithms*]

(d) (i) eg selection sort: double size of list, selection exchange: just size of list

(ii) eg selection sort n(n−1) comparisons, selection exchange n(n−1)/2 comparisons

(e) these are all "normal" data; full testing would have to include extreme/exceptional data

30. *(a)* Rainfall: array (1..20,1..12) of real or array (1..12,1..20)

(b) (i)
Algorithm or example of programming code eg:
count_months = 0
for i=1 to 12 do
    if rainfall(year,i) > 10.0 then
        count_months: = count_months + 1
    endif
endfor
set count for months to 0
repeat for each month i
    if rainfall(year,i) > 10.0 then
        add 1 to count for months
    endif
until months = 12

(ii) identify the correct loop structure (nested for) correct condition (if rainfall(j.i) > 10.0)

(c) for i=1 to 20 do
    max_month(i):=rainfall(i,l)
    for j=2 to 12 do
        if rainfall(i,j) > max_month(i) then
            max_month(i):=rainfall(i.j):
        endif
    endfor
endfor

(d) Marks must only be given for specific program changes
reference to changing array dimensions (dim array for 40 instead of 20)
reference to changing nested loops (First loop changes to 1 to 40 instead of 1 to 20)

Section III
Part D—Multimedia

31. *(a)* (i) Rapid navigation can be used through cards, pages etc
Objects can be linked together
Navigation using hyperlinks
The ability to save results for later use
Good browsing capabilities

31. (a) (continued)
    (ii) The ability to **link** media objects such as sound, video, graphics etc

  (b) (i) Staff training, typing tutors, assessment, distance learning

    (ii) Users can work at own pace, changing of direction, stopping for breaks, tally of scores given, learning at home instead of workplace

  (c) (i) DVD has higher storage capacity than CD-ROM – 4·7 to 17 Gb compared with 300 Mb to 850 Mb
This means that more media elements can be stored, thus improving presentation
It could also mean that higher quality media elements can be stored eg higher resolution, full screen video, higher frame rate etc

    (ii) 1 mark for each appropriate development with appropriate explanation:
Colour depth—millions of colours are now available
Resolution—better quality images
Refresh rate—faster, no flickering apparent to human eye
Brightness/contrast—ability to make images appear brighter or duller

    (iii) **Faster Processor**—allows programs to be loaded more quickly, calculations performed more quickly—smoother animation, faster navigation
More RAM—allows more programs and data to be loaded at any one time, leads to better quality video playback, full screen rather than small window

32. (a) Storyboard—design of each page/stage/card of multimedia presentation
Allows designer to have a clear plan of navigation routes, where multimedia elements will be positioned, how each page will be linked to another etc

  (b) **Icon based**—use of preprogrammed buttons, icons, menus which can be used to create program. Easier coding
Faster implementation, don't need programming skills
OR
Script—more flexibility with multimedia elements, more control with navigation

  (c) Scanner to input logo
Video camera—to capture frames
Video capture card—to input frames onto a computer system
Video adapter card—to allow video to be viewed on the display device

32. (continued)

  (d) Responses should include input, process and output of sound:
Sound card required for whole process (I, O and P)
Input—microphone
Process—sound manipulation software or name (Quicktime, Win Decks, Wave Studio, Waveshaper etc) **or** authoring package (Hyperstudio, Director etc)
Output—speakers (for amplification)

  (e) Minimum MPC standards allow devices to be compliant with multimedia components. Allows all devices, interfaces to work together. Minimum hardware requirements for computer to be classified as a multimedia machine

33. (a) *for 2 devices from*:
scanner, digital camera, video camera
Scanner—picture taken by "normal" camera and scanned into the computer
Digital camera/video camera—photos taken and camera connected directly to computer for input

  (b) (i) **Lossy**—compression leads to loss of information. When image is decompressed it will have less detail than original. This may still be acceptable to the human eye
Lossless—compression technique manages to encode all information so that when the image is decompressed it is exactly the same as the original. No detail is lost

    (ii) **JPEG (JPG)**—millions of colours available, common format
GIF—common format, lossless compression so original file stored
TIFF—any number of colours and options available
PNG, BMP

  (c) **Filling**—adding colours to image
Pixel editing—to remove scratches by changing colour of individual pixels
Cloning stamp—to remove scratches/blemishes/unwanted images by changing colour of pixels using another area of pixels
Special effects such as vignetting
Removing red eye, scaling, resizing, cropping and descriptions

  (d) The ability to move text and graphics freely about a page with ease
DTP packages allow graphics from a wide area of formats including TIFFs
Text Wrap—text to flow around graphics
Master pages—items on the master page will appear on all pages
Non-printing guides—to help with alignment of text and graphics

Computing Higher 2002 (contd.)

34. (a) MIDI allows for music data to be passed in both directions from the keyboard to the computer
It is a standard for musical data so that data can be passed between devices made by different manufacturers

(b) **Frequency Modulation**—sounds are generated by combining and modifying the outputs of signal generators (oscillators)
Wave Table—Digitised sound samples are stored in a table of waveforms and played at different speeds to produce different notes.

(c) (i) **Compression**—the ability to achieve a smaller file size to "shrink" files
Sampling rate—how many amplitudes are captured per second, frequency of sound readings

(ii) *accept any **one** description from*:
MIDI (.mid)—MIDI stands for Music Instruments Digital Interface; a standard for transmitting musical information between electronic instruments and computers; size of a MIDI file is small; quality of the music is very good
WAVE (.wav)—WAVE files are sound data-digital representation of an analog signal; linearly encoded; files can be large; can be stereo/mono 8/16 bit
UNLAW (.au)—the original NeXt machine sound standard. It is a digitised sound data file similar to WAVE files and takes a lot of storage space. Common on Unix/Sun platforms
MOD (.mod)—a collection of sample data and a description of how to play these samples in a certain order, pitch, and distortion on four channels; samples don't necessarily have to be from real musical instruments. The MOD format reveals a big advantage over the WAVE and MIDI formats. Any natural sound can be used as an instrument, where as MIDI can't do this. The size of a MOD file is much smaller compared to a WAVE file that produces the same sound.
AIFF (.aiff)—The Audio Interchange File Format allows one program to open a digital recording created by another program. The format actually used on CDs—though it can represent the encoded digitised sound at different sample rates.
SND (.snd)—An Amiga sound extension that is a sound data file

MP3—supported by many software applications, can be used for DVD, portable music players, web music. Compression ratio of the order of 10:1 compared to eg AIFF

(iii) **Low**—many amplitudes lost and the sound quality will be poor, not smooth and sharp
High—giant series of amplitudes taken, redundant information could be stored and hence wastage of storage space

Computing Higher 2003

SECTION I

1. Corrective – to correct errors which were not detected during testing.
Perfective – to add new features (functions) to the software.
Adaptive – to update the software to enable it to work in a new environment e.g. new OS.

2. correct – meets the specification (or fit for purpose)
reliable – how well the software operates without stopping due to design and coding faults / produces expected results at all times

3. (a) (i) structure chart, pseudocode, flowchart or any other known method

(ii) All are language independent, allow translation to different languages.
- Pseudocode useful for showing logic of single module
- structure diagram uses linked boxes showing hierarchy or shaped boxes to show constructs of program so is useful for showing overall structure and data flow
- flowchart uses shaped boxes to show constructs in the program and links to show sequence
- Pseudocode has line to line mapping with HLL – easy to convert to code

(b) Technical and user guides:
Technical
how to install software
installation requirements
User
how to operate the software, e.g. explanation of demands
tutorial guide

4. (a) Description of REPEAT or WHILE.

(b) Fixed loop is used when the number of iterations is known
Fixed loop will repeat a block of code for a fixed number of iterations

Official SQA Answers to Higher Computing

4. (continued)

(c) repeating a section of code over again

5. (a) readable code is more easily understood by other programmers
or same programmer may be maintaining at a later date

(b) Any two from:
internal documentation/commentary
meaningful variable names
structured listings / indentation/white space
modularity

6. (a) Data bus width

(b) An increase in word size increases system performance because more data can be processed in one cycle

7. Any two from:
signal a read
signal write
reset processor registers
interrupt current process
carry clock signal

8. Order of objects could be changed
Individual objects can be resized
Individual objects can be moved/edited
Objects can be resized with no loss of quality

9. rules of arithmetic are supported
two values for 0 do not exist

10. (a) (i) bus, star, ring etc

(ii) Below is a diagram of bus network topology

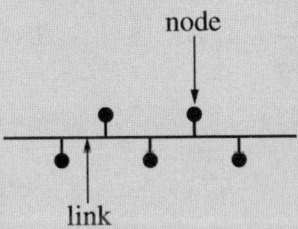

(b) Answers depend on the topology diagram given above but could include:
Bus – no communication can take place.
Ring – no communication can take place
Star – only one node is isolated

11. similarity: both are high level languages, both use modularity, both use data structures, both use control structures

difference: scripting languages are embedded within an application or OS, procedural languages stand alone

12. (a) Resolution: number of dots per inch or number of pixels used to store image
Capacity: amount of memory in the camera / number of pictures which can be stored.

(b) The higher the resolution the more memory required to store one picture so fewer pictures can be stored / capacity will need to be increased

13. Word processing: RTF, text, ASCII
Database: DBF, CSV, TAB separated
Spreadsheet: SYLK, CSV, TAB separated
Graphics: TIFF, JPEG, BMP, GIF
Audio: MP3, WAV
Web design: html
Video editing: MPEG

SECTION II

14. (a) (i) Each memory location has a unique address.

(ii) It stores the layout of memory indicating which addresses store the OS, programs and data and keeps each process separate so that overwriting does not occur.

(b) (i) If data is stored in registers within the processor then less fetches to memory are required for a process.

(ii) ALU – Adds/subtracts binary numbers. Performs logical AND, OR NOT etc.
Control Unit – manages fetching, decoding and executing of instructions

(c) (i) Contents of ROM cannot be changed.

(ii) EPROMs or EEPROMs could be used which would allow data to be erased and rewritten OR Upgraded program can be stored on new ROM chip to be inserted into machine

(iii) Advantage – Needs less power and circuitry is simpler
Disadvantage – Needs continuous signal to refresh contents of chip
Slower than SRAM

(d) $2^{32} \times 24$ bits
$\div 8 \div 1024 \div 1024 \div 1024 = 12\text{Gb}$
$12\text{Gb} - 1\text{Gb} = 11\text{Gb}$

15. (a) One possible answer could include:
Interview employees of agency, examine current paperwork, observe work place, questionnaires

(b) Answers could include any two from:
- easier to pass as a single parameter between code blocks
- easier to read/understand code than if large number of variables used
- easier to carry out list operations (search, sort etc)

Computing Higher 2003 (contd.)

15. (continued)

    (c) (i) Pass by reference is where the location/address of the variable is passed to the code block. This enables changes to the variable contents to be made and passed back out.
Pass by value is where the current value of the variable is passed into the code block, subsequent changes to that value do not affect the original variable.

    (ii) Pass by value as the search item should not be able to be changed.

  (d) All the job characteristics could be stored as facts and rules
Then the applicant's attributes could be pattern matched against the facts stored to search for the best match i.e. querying facility is "built in".

  (e) Implementation: When software is being upgraded, future programmers will have full description of how the code evolved. The function of the component parts will be clear

  Testing: Corrective maintenance is the resolution of errors not discovered at the testing stage. Documentation (e.g. test data which was used) may help to identify areas where testing was inadequate.

16. (a) DTP, Word processor with graphics capability, Integrated package
Package must allow inclusion and manipulation of text and graphics

  (b) (i) Bit depth – the number of bits used to represent the colour of a pixel, which defines the number of colours available
Type of interface – USB, parallel etc
Size of scanner surace (A3, A4, handheld etc) Scanning speed

    (ii) 6 × 4 × 600 × 600 × 8 bits
(69 120 000 bits or 8 640 000 bytes)
÷8÷1024÷1024 = 8.24 Mb

  (c) (i) Laptop – Larger RAM (128Mb) or faster processor which means more powerful applications (e.g. fully featured WP) can be used
OR larger backing storage (20Gb) so larger files/more powerful applications can be saved.
OR modem available so stories can be e-mailed to newspaper

    Palmtop – handwriting recognition software (pen-based device) used for fast input, PCMCIA slots for attaching eg modem or memory cards OR physical size allows easy portability

    (ii) Laptop – GUI (WIMP) system. Trackpad or trackerball can be used so easy to point and click. Standard keyboard useful when (large) stories have to be entered quickly.

    Palmtop – Handwriting recognition. Easy to write notes quickly (interviews, comments etc.)

  (d) Advantage: No need to create interface or searching engine, just create files, less coding required.

  Disadvantage: Lack of control over "look and feel". Lack of control over searching algorithm.

17. (a) The operating system manages and maintains the computer system. O.S. provides link between applications and hardware.

  (b) Utilities are programs that aid in the maintenance of (or enhance the use of) computer systems.
Disk formatter – formats media for use with OS
Defragmentation software – moves data around disk until it is stored in consecutive sectors
Virus checker – checks software for relevant viruses and feeds back to user

  (c) So that data elements can be used by different computers and software.

  (d) Large backing storage (Hard disc)/10GB+ – to ensure storage of OS
High processing power 500MHz+ – to ensure computer runs fast enough when carrying out other tasks.

  (e) (i) The program is split into appropriate units therefore it is easier for the programmer to find relevant parts of the OS which are linked to the new features
OR
the new code could be tried and tested on its own.
OR
Different programmers can work on different modules

    (ii) Test data which 'exercises' all program paths and special cases. All 3 types of test data must be mentioned.
Program is tested by typical users for real world exposure (beta testing)

18. (a) Robustness: A is more error prone as user may mistype the name, B – invalid entries not possible
Ease of data entry: A requires keyboard skills, B is able to be used by people with poor computer skills because no keyboard skills would be needed
Efficiency of Resources: A is not memory or processor intensive, B uses more memory/processor power to draw the menus etc

18 (continued)

(b)
- standard routines for the creation of buttons
- linking of buttons to segments of code
- any other valid point

(c)
- use of subroutines to allow easier conversion
- sparse or no use of processor specific code
- use of different compilers to create different versions of object code
- meaningful variable names to allow conversion

(d) A module library is a set of pre-written routines which can be re-used
Module components have already been pre-tested

(e) set occurrences = 0
FOR position = 1 to maxarray
IF tree$(position) = target$
THEN increment occurrences
NEXT position
Display occurrences
(REPEAT could be used instead of FOR)

19.

(a) (i) Global: variables which can be used by any part of the program.
Local: scope of the variable is limited to the procedure in which it is used

(ii) Local variables cannot be accidentally changed by other parts of the software. Their use makes the behaviour of the code more predictable.

(b) Any three from:
- intended platform for software
- suitability of type ie Prolog in AI application, assembler etc
- data types available in language
- features/constructs within language
- support tools available i.e. CASE
- any other valid point

(c) array of strings
Or string array or (2D) array of char.

(d) set position to 0
set current position to 1
loop until end of list OR position >0
if name at current position = window name
set position to current position
end if
add 1 to current position
end loop

(e) An example of a possible answer is:
Input/Output subsystem will take mouse clicks and pass data to a relevant part of the program

SECTION III – PART A Artificial Intelligence

20.

(a) (i) Parallel processing allows several clauses or rules to be processed simultaneously so improving overall processing time.
Improvements to backing storage have meant that more information could be included in the knowledge base.
Improvements to internal memory have meant that larger knowledge bases can be manipulated.
Faster clock speeds have improved processing time so more could be expected from MYCIN.

(ii) Any actions taken as a result of using the expert systems are at the users risk.

A good explanatory interface will give justification of how a result is obtained and will help the user to evaluate the worth of the advice.

(iii) Many copies of the expert system can be made and distributed, rather than just the few human experts.
Expert not always at the point of need.
Advice is always consistent whereas human experts may be inconsistent
Combines knowledge of many experts.
Can be used in training to confirm learner's knowledge.
MYCIN does not forget things.

(b) Concept of knowledge engineer going back to domain expert for clarification / more information / checking etc after first consultation in order to proceed with the development of the system
OR
Different domain experts may give conflicting advice so need to go back to confirm advice

(c) Many definitions of AI (or many types of intelligent behaviour) and each gives rise to a particular field of research.

Also idea that it is easier to focus on making a machine (or application) which can perform a specific (AI) task than it is to create a "thinking machine".

21.

(a) (i) No or false

(ii) There is no information about Macdonald so to take the result that Macdonald is male is misleading.

(b) Establish a match for female(friedland) at line 12,
try to establish sub-goal male(friedland)
subgoal fails
so not(male(friedland)) succeeds

(c) boss(grainger,W) AND female(W)

(d) same_department(X,Y) if is_manager_of(Z,X) and is_manager_of(Z,Y)

Computing Higher
2003 (contd.)

21. (continued)

(e) (i) Recursion in line 14 needs a terminating condition which is provided by line 13.

(ii) If lines 13 and 14 are the other way round the terminator would not be encountered by the search so the recursion would go on forever.

22. (a) Reasons could include:
a limited number of simple rules which were straight forward to code
limited computer technology meant anything more complicated would give processing / memory problems
game playing requires intelligence by people so was a good beginning for computer emulation (mixture of reasoning and creativity)

(b) Computer may be programmed to follow strategies like a human player (use of heuristics).
Computer may be programmed to learn from mistakes like a human player.
Human player may not be very good at the game and so may play randomly like a poorly programmed computer.

(c) (i) Pieces need to be turned right way up
Detail must not be 'lost' in cutting of the jig-saw
'Picture' for comparison needs to be a full size identical copy
Position of camera
Camera angle

(ii) Identification of corners first and then edges…
to give a smaller number of pieces to search
to build up framework of jig-saw
OR group like coloured pieces and join groups together.

(d) Computer vision (linked to pattern matching) is needed for reduction of wastage, adaptability in jobs, freedom of mobility
Parallel processing to improve speed of processing of instructions

23. (a) Databases have rigid structure (records), facts and rules in knowledge bases are less well defined.
Databases produce results to simple/complex searches whilst the logic applied to a knowledge base allows for deductions to be made.

(b) Logic processes are independent of subject content of knowledge base
OR
single inference engine can be used with different knowledge bases

(c) Knowledge engineer – organises the knowledge of the expert into a form suitable for computer processing.

(d) (i) A certainty factor is a number which is attached to an advice rule to reflect degree of belief that advice, based on information provided, is correct

(ii) More than one alternative piece of advice, each with a certainty factor can be offered
Answers may also give a description of a particular situation involving several advice rules with certainty factors from any expert system shell

(e) (i) Examples:
Forward chaining:
IF hair IS brown AND
Face shape IS oval AND
Eye colour IS blue
THEN name IS Jenny

Backward chaining:
ADVISE name IS Jenny IF
Hair IS brown AND
Face shape IS oval AND
Eye colour IS blue

(ii) Forward chaining: prognosis, monitoring or control systems
planning + classification

(iii) Backward chaining: diagnostic problems, giving advice

SECTION III Part B - Computer Networking

24. (a) (i) peer-to-peer: each station on the network has the same status and can share files.
client-server: only certain computers on the network can make resources available to other stations.

(ii) All shared files stored on a central server means data more likely to be up to date and correct – everyone using the same data.
The security (access rights) of a central server can be controlled centrally so files are more secure.
Easier to backup centrally stored files.

(b) Telephone link uses modem which is slower (lower band width) than internal ethernet / communication channels.
Home computer less powerful than company computers.

(c) firewall computer is a security device to prevent unauthorised access (hacking) into a network e.g.
- a firewall computer will only transfer packets for particular ports.
- a firewall computer may accept / reject packets from certain IP addresses

Official SQA Answers to Higher Computing

24. (continued)

(d) A hacker who discovers a user's password cannot dial in from another telephone number.
Links can only be made to specific numbers.
Data is safer as it is guaranteed to be delivered to a private address.
User does not pay for telephone call.

25. (a) (i) Router

(ii) determines most efficient path for sending message to ultimate destination
bridges can't connect geographically distant networks, routers work with phone line or ISDN
all of the LAN's are using TCP/IP

(b) TCP breaks down the data into packets and adds header(s)
IP delivers to receiver
TCP re-assembles packets in correct order.

(c) Large bandwidth, large buffering capacity to cope with size of sound and video files.

(d) Can queue jobs and deal with them by priority
Can direct print jobs to particular printers
Can store print jobs until they are printed.

(e) • Standard protocol which enables communication between different platforms
- works with whatever network cabling is already installed in the building
- isn't tied to one particular hardware or software vendor
- can be used on LAN to create private internet i.e. use of e-mail, browsers on LAN.

26. (a) Computer networks give access to large amounts of shared information.
Individuals or societies who do not have access to computer networks will not have the same access to information and so will be information poor.

(b) Different laws in different countries makes it hard for authorities to work together
Which country's law should be used—the one where the user is or the one where the host computer is?

(c) (i) protocol – method used to transfer resource e.g. ftp, http, mail
host_address – address of computer which holds the resource
resource name – file name or pathname of resource on the host computer

(ii) e.g. http://www.anyhost.com/news/index.html
protocol – http,
host_address – www.anyhost.com,
resource name – /news/index.html

26. (continued)

(d) (i) circuit switching

(ii) packets broken down into the same size enables efficient storage management, allows the small packet to be sent by whatever route is convenient at the time, so that transmission appears to be quicker, other messages can be inserted when there are any gaps in transmission of small packets.

27. (a) (i) modem and communications software

(ii) software – controls modem, encodes data, manages data flow

(b) (i) Real time audio and visual communication of several people in different places anywhere with network connection, whiteboard utility allows greater interactivity.

(ii) By encrypting the signal on the network.

(c) (i) JPEG or any other acceptable, e.g. TIFF, GIF, PNG

(ii) JPEG compressed file format able to represent large range of colours and resolutions.
GIF – lossless compression

(d) Any two layers from:
- Physical layer: addresses physical characteristics of the network, e.g. cabling, connectors etc
- Data link layer: addresses size of packet, means of addressing packet, preventing two nodes transmitting at same time
- Network layer: routes packets from one network to another
- Transport layer: gives each node unique address, manages connections between nodes
- Session layer: makes sure sessions are established and maintained
- Presentation layer: converts data sent over network from one type of representation to another, e.g. apply and remove compression
- Application layer: techniques that application programs use to communicate with the network, network OS works within this layer

Section III Part C – Computer Programming

28. (a) Array of integers

(b) current top of stack/stack pointer
the maximum size of the array

Computing Higher 2003 (contd.)

28. (continued)

(c) Diagram or explanation should show:
- the array as a group of contiguous storage locations
- pointer to the last item of the list (top)
- space for adding the new item beyond
- incrementing the pointer to the new end item (top=top+1)
- the new item placed at the end (array(top)=new item)

(d) (i)
```
FOR current = 1 to (arraymax-1)
  FOR count = (current+1) to arraymax
    IF array(current) > array(count) THEN
      let dummy = array(current)
      let array(current) = array(count)
      let array(count) = dummy
    END IF
  NEXT
NEXT
```
(Many other algorithms are possible.)

(ii) <u>Selection sort</u>
uses a second array of same size therefore doubles memory requirement (2n locations) repeatedly finds the smallest item in the list and copies it into the current position (n squared)

<u>Exchange sort</u>
memory efficient (uses n + 1 locations) compares current element with rest of list, swapping smaller items into current. Then applies same to rest of list (n squared – n)

29. (a) (i) Array subscript error (reading past end of file is also acceptable)

(ii) Use a conditional loop which detects the end of the file and/or array

(b)
```
set count = 1
WHILE NOT end of data AND count <= arraymax
  READ name$(count),hours(count)
  count = count + 1
LOOP
```

(c) Using the following code example for illustrative purposes:
```
FOR count = 1 TO 1000
  PRINT count; "squared is";count*count
NEXT count
```

<u>Compiler</u>
All three lines are decoded once then the resultant object code is executed ie the print line is decoded once and executed 1000 times.

<u>Interpreter</u>
All three lines are decoded then executed in turn ie the print line is decoded and executed 1000 times. This is 999 more translations of the print line.

(d) Note: This section shuffles up the remaining elements in both arrays and blanks the last item in the lists

```
FOR count = position to maxarray-1
  name$(count) = name$(count+1)
  hours(count) = hours(count+1)
NEXT count
name$(maxarray) = ""
hours(maxarray) = 0
maxarray = maxarray – 1
```

30. (a) Counting Occurrences (Conditional Loop and Count are also acceptable)

(b) Dry run is the manual execution of code using pen, paper and structured test data
Carried out to check the logic of code block

(c) This allows the modules to be incorporated into the program as "black boxes", much in the same way as modules in a library
Testing can be carried out by more than one programmer

(d) <u>Trace tables</u>:
Table of variables with current values. These allow the programmer to monitor the behaviour of individual variables and help prevent errors and unexpected side-effects.

<u>Break points</u>:
Points in the program where execution will pause. This helps the programmer to identify the position of errors.

(e) (i) $128 * 0.05 = 6.4$ seconds

(ii) $128 = 2^7$, 8 comparisons.
$8 * 0.05 = 0.4$ seconds

(iii) A binary search requires the file to be sorted.

31. (a) Any reasonable description of a section of pre-written code available for use by programmers.

(b)
```
set sum = 0
FOR digit = 1 TO 10
  sum = sum + scanned(digit)
NEXT digit
set checksum = REMAINDER(sum,9)
IF checksum = scanned(maxarray) THEN
  report VALID
ELSE prompt for rescan
```

(c) Any reasonable description of the use of a utility for line-by-line scanning of code for logic, or runtime, errors by programmer
More detail should be given regarding the reporting of variable values etc.

31. (continued)

(d) (i) Examples of two difficulties are:
deletion from only one array results in wrong calculation of product numbers
sorting of arrays must be in parallel if numbers are to remain associated with correct items
any other valid point

(ii) Two alternatives might be 2D array or records
Note: Advantage should be clearly expressed

Section III – Part D Multimedia

32. (a) (i) icon-based – use of preprogrammed buttons, icons or menus
script-based – input from keyboard to create commands

(ii) Icon-based – no commands need to be remembered, easier to create presentations using graphical images etc.
Script-based – more flexibility as user is not restricted to pre-given tools

(b) (i) MPC standards describe the minimum hardware specification requirements that a computer must have in order to be classified as a multimedia machine.

(ii) Any from:
64+Mb RAM, 333+MHz processor, backing storage (CD-R, CD-RW, Hard Disc), CD-ROMs (600kps), sound card (16-bit, MIDI playback), video (640x480x64).

(c) (i) Hypertext system allows the navigation of text using links – fundamental feature of WWW.

(ii) Compression reduces file size which reduces download time (and storage space).

(iii) Description of copyright laws as relevant to copying elements.

33. (a) Any three from:
Scaling – the image can be pulled or squeezed
Filling – using solid colours or patterns to fill in a shape
Clipping/Cropping – taking out unimportant detail from image
Morphing – joining two images together showing the transformation from one to the other
Smearing – rubbing over to produce a smudging effect
Blending – to mix different colours together
Gamma correction – changes brightness and ratios of colours.

(b) (i) JPEG, GIF, TIFF, BMP

33. (continued)

(ii) JPEG – millions of colours can be used, common format, small size due to compression.
GIF – common format, lossless compression so original file stored as small file size.
TIFF – any number of colours and options available
BMP – Windows standard, uncompressed

(c) (i) CD-R or CD-RW (CD-ROM or CD not asscceptable) – common backing storage device can be used by clients, can store up to 850 Mb, durable, cheap and lightweight, portable
DVD-R (not DVD) – large storage up to 20Gb, faster access than CD

(ii) Wrong OS, not enough RAM, files saved in wrong format, no appropriate software on client's machine

34. (a) (i) Camera (or video digitiser) connected to computer via video capture card
Analogue to digital conversion required
Compression (MPEG) must be used before the frames can be saved

(ii) No analogue to digital conversion required, quality improved, faster to capture.

(b) (i) Fewer frames – less storage required but jerky motion.

(ii) More frames – smoother motion but more storage required.

(c) (i) Any two from:
Clips can be cropped
Frames can be deleted
Timeline can be used to change frames around
Transitions can be used to make video more interesting (fade in/out, dissolve, ripple etc)
Sound can be edited, removed or created

(ii) RAM – 128Mb + so that the clips can be viewed
Backing storage – 20Gb+ (video projects are large files even under compression)
Processor – 500MHz+ to ensure computer can cope with large projects with many frames.

35. (a) Lossy compression leads to a loss of information whereas lossless compression encodes data so that the original file can be recreated in its entirety.

(b) Text document is scanned to produce a bit map
A group of pixels are pattern matched against character (bit maps) stored within the OCR software
When a match is found the character's ASCII code is stored in a text output file

Computing Higher
2003 (contd.)

28. (continued)

(c) ASCII (Plain text) – each character is stored but no formatting information is stored.
RTF (Rich Text Format) – formatting information (text font, size, style etc) is stored as well as the text itself.

(d) (i) Sampled – naturally occurring sounds
Synthesised – computer-generated sounds

(ii) Any two from:
Recording of sound into digitized data for future use
Playback of digitized sound
Allows connection of microphone, speakers, MIDI equipment
FM Synthesis where digitized sounds are generated mimicking natural sounds.

Official SQA answers to 1-84372-120-1
SQP, 2000, 2001, 2002, 2003 exams

HIGHER SPECIMEN QUESTION PAPER

[C017/SQP009]

Higher Computing

Time: 2½ hours

NATIONAL QUALIFICATIONS

Specimen Question Paper

Attempt **all** questions in Section I.

Attempt **four** questions in Section II
    Question 1 and Question 2
    and **either** Question 3 **or** Question 4
    and **either** Question 5 **or** Question 6

Attempt **one** Sub-Section of Section III. In this Section there are four Sub-Sections, one for each of the Optional Units

    Computer Programming — *Page seven*
    Artificial Intelligence   — *Page ten*
    Computer Networking — *Page thirteen*
    Multimedia Technology — *Page fifteen*

For the Optional Unit chosen, attempt
    Question 1 and Question 2
    and **either** Question 3 **or** Question 4.

Note: for Multimedia Technology, attempt Questions 1 to 5 and **either** Question 6 **or** Question 7.

Read all questions carefully.

Write your answers in the two answer books provided. One answer book should be used for Sections I and II and the second answer book **must** be used for Section III.

Do not write on the question paper.

Write as neatly as possible.

SECTION I

Attempt all questions in this section

1. Name a software development environment with which you are familiar. Give an example of a *complex condition* in your software development environment. — 2

2. State **three** characteristics you would expect to find in a well designed HCI. — 3

3. Design notation is an essential tool within a design methodology that is used to represent software design. Describe, by means of an example, **two** design notations with which you are familiar. — 4

4. The software development process is described as being *iterative*. State what is meant by this term. — 1

5. A program is to be written that will read in a list of student marks, check that each mark is within an acceptable range, and determine the highest mark.

   Which **two** of the following algorithms will be used in this program?

   Counting occurrences
   Minimum
   Linear search
   Input validation
   Find Maximum — 2

6. Describe a situation where an error would be generated from the operating system during the run-time of a program. — 1

7. At the end of a sponsored walk, all the contestant data is entered into a file. Which algorithm from the list below will be required to evaluate the slowest time taken to complete the walk?

   Counting occurrences
   FindMinimum
   Linear search
   Input validation
   Maximum

   Give a reason for your answer. — 2

8. (a) One method of representing a negative integer in a computer is by using the two's complement of the corresponding positive integer.

   Which of the following is the 8 bit two's complement representation of −7?
   (i) 00000111
   (ii) 10000111
   (iii) 11111001 — 1

   (b) Describe **one** way of storing a real number in computer memory. — 1

9. A small business buys a desktop computer system with a multi-scanning monitor and a scanner.
    (a) What main feature distinguishes a multi-scanning monitor from a single frequency monitor? **1**
    (b) The scanner is used to scan a 5 in by 7 in photograph at 600 dpi in 256 colours.
        (i) How much memory would be required to store the scanned image?
        (ii) Name **two** storage devices which could be used to store the image. **3**
    (c) The desktop computer has an operating system which uses a GUI.
        Describe **three** characteristics of this type of interface. **3**
    (d) The desktop computer is to be connected to a network.
        (i) What hardware needs to be installed in the computer?
        (ii) Describe one network topology which might be used in an office. **2**

10. (a) Give **one** example of a communications protocol. **1**
    (b) Why are protocols necessary in computer communications? **1**

11. Programming languages may be classified by the type of problem which they are designed to solve.
    (a) Name **two** programming languages which are designed to solve different types of problem. For **each** language, state the type of problem it is designed to solve. **1**
    (b) Give an example of the use of a scripting language in a GPP. **1**

(30)

[END OF SECTION I]

SECTION II

Attempt FOUR questions in this Section

Question 1 and Question 2
and either Question 3 or Question 4
and either Question 5 or Question 6

Marks

1. A microcomputer has a 300 MHz processor, 64 MBytes of RAM, serial, parallel and USB interfaces and a 6 GByte hard disk. It is used to create on-line tutorials for software packages.

   (a) State **two** reasons why a computer needs interfaces to connect peripheral devices to the processor. **2**

   (b) Clock speed is not the only way to express the throughput of this computer.

   Explain how each of the following can affect the throughput of this computer:

   (i) amount of memory installed;

   (ii) choice of hard disk drive. **3**

   (c) A printer has to be added to the system. State **two** characteristics of a printer which you would consider when making a purchase. Explain why your chosen characteristics are important. **2**

   (d) The computer system is to be used to create on-line tutorials for software packages.

   (i) Suggest **two** types of software which might be used for creating on-line tutorials.

   (ii) State the purpose of your chosen software. **3**

2. A security system is to be developed for a local insurance company. Each employee will be issued with a security card upon which will be encoded their personal details and a four digit Personal Identification Number (PIN). A photograph of the employee will also be displayed on each card.

   When keyed in, the PIN will be used by the system to check access rights to particular sections of the insurance building.

   The design of the security card is illustrated below.

   ULTRASAFE INSURANCE

   Name: A Person
   Designation: A Job Type
   Security Section: Section Code

   Employee Image of 1 square inch

   (a) List, in correct order, the stages involved in the development of software for this security system. **2**

   (b) Identify **two** distinct objects and their corresponding operations that will be needed to produce the security cards. **2**

   (c) It is particularly important that the security system is reliable. State what is meant by the term *reliable*. **1**

   (d) At the design stage, it is decided that a database will hold all employee information. The company currently employs 650 people.

   (i) Suggest a suitable input device that could be used to digitise the employee photograph.

   (ii) The selected digitiser produces an image of 300 dpi resolution and 256 levels of grey scale. Calculate the amount of storage required to hold the employee photograph. State clearly any assumptions that you make. **3**

   (e) Suggest **two** further measures that could be taken to increase security and, for each measure, identify any additional hardware or software requirements. **2**

Attempt either Question 3 or Question 4

3. The structured chart below represents a section of a stock control system. The stock control system operates by increasing or decreasing stock levels according to information held in a stock transaction file. The stock transaction file contains a unique identifier for each stock item and an indicator of whether the stock should be increased or decreased in level.

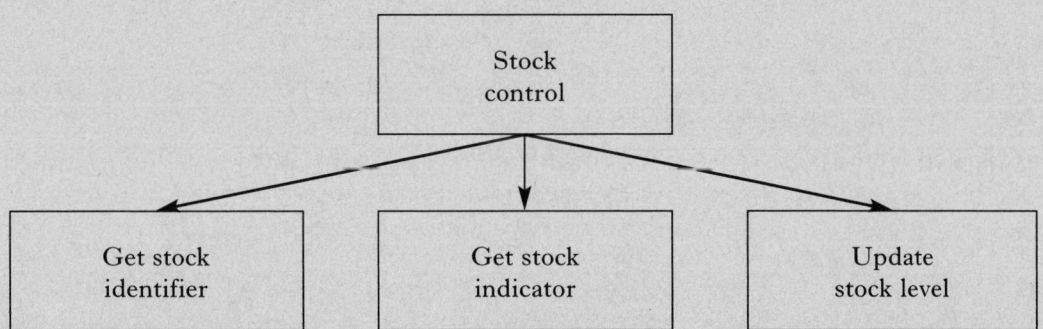

   (a) A module is written for each of the processes labelled in the above structured diagram. Each module will make use of parameter passing. Explain how the use of parameter passing can improve the portability of the software. **2**

   (b) For each of the modules, Get stock identifier, Get stock indicator and Update stock level, identify the type(s) of parameter that would be needed. **4**

   (c) When testing software it is desirable to use systematic testing. Describe the steps that you would take to systematically test the stock control program above. **2**

   (d) A 16 bit computer is used to develop this program. The stock code is represented as an integer in the high level language used. What is the maximum stock code value that can be represented in this system? State any assumptions that you make. **2**

4. At Strictview Academy, students are awarded an overall course pass or fail. They need to achieve at least fifty percent (50%) in all examinations to get a course pass. This is illustrated in the table below.

Name	Mark 1	Mark 2	Mark 3	Result
Jane	32	52	60	Fail
James	45	67	83	Fail
John	52	63	65	Pass
			Total Passes	1

   The Head of Department asks you to develop a computerised solution to this problem.

   (a) Identify **two** distinct objects and their corresponding operations required to solve the problem above. **2**

   (b) Name a software development environment with which you are familiar. Describe how the complex condition required to determine a course pass would be written in the software development environment you have named. **2**

   (c) The solution to this problem could be developed in a High Level Language. Alternatively a higher level language such as a Fourth Generation Language or a General Purpose Package could be used.

   Compare and contrast the use of a High Level Language and a higher level language to solve the problem at Strictview Academy. Your answer should refer to:
   - customisation of the user interface;
   - input validation. **4**

   (d) Outline a counting occurrences algorithm that would determine the Total Passes in the table above. You may write the algorithm in textual or graphical form. **2**

Attempt either Question 5 or Question 6

Marks

5. (a) List **four** functions of a single user operating system. 2

   (b) Most modern microcomputers have an operating system which supports multitasking.

   (i) Explain why multitasking is required in modern microcomputers.

   (ii) What additional functions must an operating system have in order to support multitasking? 4

   (c) Describe in detail the processes carried out by a network operating system when a user logs on at a microcomputer on a local area network. 4

6. A computer system has been created which allows the user to keep a record of bills which have been paid to various companies. Details of each bill are entered using the following input screen organisation.

Screen 1

Date	3/5/99
Company	T H Jones
Item	Electrical
Amount	£ 50·99

A list of all payments to the same company are then displayed as follows.

Screen 2

Date	Company	Item	Amount
5/6/99	British Telecom	Phone Bill	£ 108·00
3/3/99	British Telecom	Phone Bill	£ 110·00
20/2/99	British Telecom	Install extra line	£ 45·00
		Total	£ 263·00

(a) Database software has been used to implement this system. Describe **two** features of database software which have been illustrated in the above diagram. 2

(b) It was intended that the list in screen 2 should have been arranged in order of date. This has not happened even though the computer operator sorted on the date field.

Explain why the list might not have been sorted as required. 2

(c) The users of the system would like it to be expanded to include more facilities. It has been suggested that a High Level Language be used to create a new program which would satisfy all the users' needs.

Give **one** advantage and **one** disadvantage of using a High Level Language to develop a solution to this problem. 2

(d) (i) At what stage in the software development process would the developers decide on whether to use a High Level Language?

   (ii) What information would a developer need to help make this decision? 2

(e) After the new system is developed, information from old files will need to be transferred to the new system. Describe how the use of standard data formats would help in this process. 2

[END OF SECTION II]

SECTION III

Attempt ONE of the Optional Units in this Section

SECTION III—Computer Programming

**Attempt Question 1 and Question 2
and either Question 3 or Question 4**

Marks

1. Software development environments offer a range of tools to support the programmer.
   - (a) A text editor, rather than a word processor, is used to alter program code. Describe **two** features of a dedicated text editor *not found in a word processor* that would support the editing of a program. **2**
   - (b) Give an example of a language in each of the following classes:
     - (i) imperative language;
     - (ii) declarative language;
     - (iii) a language embedded in an application package;
     - (iv) object-oriented language. **2**
   - (c) Describe how the following are used to detect errors in program code:
     - (i) a trace debugging tool;
     - (ii) breakpoints. **4**
   - (d) Compare the use of paper based debugging tools, such as a trace table, with on-line tools such as a trace facility. **2**

2. Data structures allow problems to be modelled so that data processing can be carried out efficiently.
   - (a) Describe the data structures *queue* and *stack*. **2**
   - (b) The stack data structure is associated with two main operations, pop and push. Describe in pseudocode or in another suitable form, the pop operation. **3**
   - (c) Describe **one** situation where a queue data structure could be used, and **one** situation where a stack data structure could be used. **2**
   - (d) Sequential files can be stored on magnetic disc or magnetic tape. These files can then be searched for particular values.

     Explain how you would choose between a linear search or a binary search if you were required to search for an item in a sequential file. **3**

Computer Programming (continued)

Attempt either Question 3 or Question 4

Marks

3. HStill Academy has 2050 pupils. All pupil data is held centrally and can be accessed for a variety of purposes. Here is an example of a pupil record in record card format.

    Forename   Fred
    Surname   Smith
    Date of Birth   10.2.84
    Class   3A3
    Course   English, Maths, French, Computing, Latin

    (a) (i) State **two** methods of representing the date of birth information in a program.

    (ii) Explain which of these methods would be more efficient of processor time if two records were being compared. **4**

    (b) The records must frequently be searched on the Surname field. The entire set of pupil data is held in main memory for this operation. The binary search algorithm is used for the search operation.

    (i) What conditions must be satisfied by the data if a binary search algorithm is used for the search operation?

    (ii) Outline in pseudocode (or in some suitable form) the structure of the binary search algorithm in this case. **4**

    (c) Name **two** sort algorithms which could be used to sort this data while it is held in a main memory. Compare these algorithms in terms of their efficiency in the use of memory and of processor time. **2**

Marks

Computer Programming (continued)

4. A college requires a program to process test results for classes of students. Classes consist of up to 40 students.

   Here is a sample of the input data. Data will be input from the keyboard.

Student Code	Test 1	Test 2	Test 3	Test 4	Test 5	Test 6	Test 7	Test 8
1004	23	19	−1	79	−1	6	47	−1
1234	0	90	89	78	54	67	−1	23
1579	50	50	51	80	91	50	52	29
1921	87	100	89	76	93	67	56	50

   Results for each test are in the range 0–100, representing the scores achieved. A result of −1 indicates that the student did not sit a test.

   The final grade is decided in the following way.

   If the student has sat at least 6 tests, the final result is the average of the tests sat with grades being awarded according to the following table:

Result	Grade
0–39	6
40–49	5
50–59	4
60–69	3
70–79	2
80–100	1

   If the student has sat less than 6 tests, Result is set to −1 and a final grade of 7 is awarded.

   It is required to produce three files. A Raw Data file which contains a copy of the input data, a Results file which contains the students' numbers and grades, and a Text file which contains lines of the following format:

   Student 1004 has achieved a grade 7
   Student 1234 has achieved a grade 4.

   Several data structures are required to solve this problem along with file handling.

   (a) Describe how
      (i) a two dimensional array and
      (ii) an array of records

   could be used to store this information in main memory. You may illustrate your answer with a variable or type declaration in a language with which you are familiar. **2**

   (b) Which representation would allow the programmer to produce more readable code? Explain your answer. **1**

   (c) Describe how the calculation of a student's grade would be carried out for **one** of the two representations mentioned in part (a). You may use pseudocode or program code if you wish. **4**

   (d) State which of these representations will allow the writing of the Raw Data file to be carried out with greater efficiency in terms of processor time. Explain your answer. **3**

SECTION III—Artificial Intelligence

**Attempt Question 1 and Question 2
and either Question 3 or Question 4**

Marks

1. (a) Three main components of an expert system are the knowledge base, the inference engine and the explanatory interface. Describe the function of each component. **3**

   (b) An expert system is being developed to help members of expeditions in remote tropical regions to diagnose and treat medical conditions. The expert system is to be built using rules such as:

   IF temperature > 36
       AND skin colour is orange
       AND symptoms include weakness
           THEN problem might be Orange Marsh fever

   (i) In this rule, the words "might be" indicate that there is some doubt about the diagnosis. How could the rule be adapted to deal with this? **1**

   (ii) Rules are not the only way to represent knowledge in an expert system. Describe one other way of representing the knowledge contained in the above rule. **2**

   (iii) Once the knowledge engineer has implemented the expert system, what further stages in the development process would be required before the software could be released commercially? **2**

   (iv) Advice rules suggesting appropriate treatment will also be added to the expert system. Write advice rules to represent the following information.

   "The best treatment for Orange Marsh fever is 25 mg of orthomyolite 3 times daily, or 15 mg if the patient is under 16 or over 70." **2**

Marks

Artificial Intelligence (continued)

2. (a) A programmer is developing software to solve a problem in Artificial Intelligence. She could choose to use a declarative language (like Prolog) or an algorithmic language (like Pascal).

    (i) How is knowledge represented in a declarative language?

    (ii) Why is a declarative language particularly appropriate for solving AI problems? **3**

   (b) The following is part of a knowledge base about Europe.

   ```
   1   is_in (paris france)
   2   is_in (berlin germany)
   3   is_in (vienna austria)
   4   is_in (london england)
   5   is_in (edinburgh scotland)
   6   is_in (scotland uk)
   7   is_in (england uk)

   8   currency (france franc)
   9   currency (germany mark)
   10  currency (austria schilling)
   11  currency (uk pound)

   12  can_use (Y X) if currency (X Y)
   13  can_use (Y X) if is_in (X Z)
       and can_use (Y Z)
   ```

   At the moment, the program will not fully answer the query

   `is_in (X uk)`

   as a human might expect.

   (i) Explain why the program will not answer this query correctly.

   (ii) Write down **one rule** which could be added to the program which would enable the program to find all solutions to the above query. **2**

   (c) Assuming that a depth first search is used, explain how the program would find the solution to the query **3**

   `can_use (pound scotland)`

   (d) Explain why the program **cannot** find solutions to the query

   `NOT (can_use (pound X))` **2**

Artificial Intelligence (continued)

Attempt either Question 3 or Question 4

Marks

3. The ability to understand "natural language" is one aspect of human intelligence which Artificial Intelligence (AI) researchers have attempted to model.
   - (a) State **two** other aspects of human intelligence which Artificial Intelligence (AI) research has attempted to model. **1**
   - (b) Describe the difference between natural language processing and voice recognition. **2**
   - (c) Describe a practical application of natural language processing. **2**
   - (d) Describe **two** difficulties which are encountered when attempting to implement natural language processing. **2**
   - (e) Hardware developments have allowed some areas of AI research to become more successful over the last 10 years. Describe **one** such hardware development, and explain how it has contributed to the success of a particular area of AI research. **3**

4. Pattern recognition is an important area of development in Artificial Intelligence.
   - (a) State **one** application area where pattern recognition of visual input is used. **1**
   - (b) State **one** application area where pattern recognition of sound input is used. **1**
   - (c) Describe how system hardware constraints can limit the effectiveness of computer based pattern recognition. **2**
   - (d) Describe how the input data can affect the effectiveness of computer based pattern recognition. **2**
   - (e) A pattern recognition application will probably use some brute force search method to search its database. Describe briefly **one** brute force search method, and explain how heuristics could be used to improve the efficiency of the search. **4**

SECTION III—Computer Networking

**Attempt Question 1 and Question 2
and <u>either</u> Question 3 <u>or</u> Question 4**

Marks

1. Doctors in a health centre are considering installation of a local area network. There will be a terminal in each of the six doctors' rooms and one computer in the administrator's office. Each terminal will have access to the local hospital's database and its on-line medical information system. The network must allow for future expansion.

   (a) A bus topology and a star topology are being considered.

   For each topology, state **one** advantage and **one** disadvantage in this situation.   **2**

   (b) The doctors often require access to worldwide on-line information systems.

      (i) Explain why a gateway may be required to enable this access.

      (ii) Give **two** reasons why medical personnel might consider it worthwhile to subscribe to such on-line systems.   **3**

   (c) The doctors hope to make use of video conferencing facilities once the network is established.

   Describe the term *video conferencing*. Your description should include details about the transmission media and multimedia hardware required.   **3**

   (d) Explain why video conferencing gives better results when used with a point to point direct connection rather than by using the Internet.   **2**

2. (a) State the meaning of the term "internetwork".   **1**

   (b) Name a piece of equipment which is required in an "internetwork" but not in a network.   **1**

   (c) International data transmission standards are necessary when designing communication systems.

      (i) Explain why there is a need for international data transmission standards.   **2**

      (ii) Describe **two** benefits which might arise from **not** adopting international standards.   **2**

   (d) The OSI model is a standard for computer to computer dialogue which divides the communications process into seven layers. Describe the functions carried out by:

      (i) the transport layer;

      (ii) the network layer.   **4**

Computer Networking (continued)

Attempt either Question 3 or Question 4

Marks

3. Some companies set up intranets, rather than allowing workers direct access to the Internet.
   (a) State **one** advantage and **one** disadvantage for the company of using an intranet rather than the Internet. **2**
   (b) What is the purpose of a network operating system? **1**
   (c) Describe the following terms in the context of an intranet:
      (i) peer to peer network;
      (ii) client server relationship;
      (iii) distributed processing. **3**
   (d) "Communications systems are impersonal and mean that less human contact is experienced."
   Discuss this view giving **two** points for and **two** points against. **4**

4. (a) Describe how a firewall is used to provide security for a school network which is directly connected to the Internet. **3**
   (b) Explain what is meant by the URL

   `ftp://ftp.somesite.sch.uk/names.doc` **3**

   (c) Describe in technical detail how a file is transferred between two computers on a network using the TCP/IP protocol. **4**

SECTION III—Multimedia Technology

**Attempt all Questions on this page
and <u>either</u> Question 6 <u>or</u> Question 7**

Marks

1. Describe how data is stored and organised on a CD-ROM. You should mention how the system is designed to cope with small defects in the fragile medium. **4**

2. When you attempt to scan a black and white clip art item using a flatbed scanner at 2400×2400 dpi resolution, the resulting image is almost entirely white. There is no fault in the hardware.

    (a) State **two** reasons why the image has not been captured as you might have hoped, and describe how you could use the scanner software to correct the problem. **4**

    (b) Text capture using a scanner is one method of text input. There can be problems with this method, even when the text image is scanned correctly. Describe **two** problems which are associated with this method of text capture. **2**

3. Name **two** facilities which you would expect to find in a professional Desktop Publishing package but not in a full-featured Word Processing package. **2**

4. When elements of a multimedia presentation are printed to a laser printer for distribution to the audience, images must be transformed so that they can be printed using a black and white (not grey scale) output device.

    Outline how this process is carried out by the computer software. **3**

5. An Educational software company wishes to produce a language learning package with the following facilities:
    - display of text in English and in the language being learned
    - display of still graphical images in multiple colours
    - short video and audio sequences to demonstrate the language being learned
    - the ability to have the user repeat spoken phrases and to have this compared with the original so that they can have feedback on their progress.

    Specify **in technical detail** a computer system which could **readily** support such an application. **5**

Multimedia Technology (continued)

Attempt either Question 6 or Question 7

Marks

6. JPEG and GIF are common file formats used for graphic images. Both use a form of data compression.
   (a) State the types of graphic image to which each format is best suited. **1**
   (b) Outline the method of data compression used in **either** JPEG **or** GIF format files. **2**

   Music is an important part of multimedia.
   (c) Describe how music data is represented:
       (i) in a MIDI file;
       (ii) in a file containing music captured using a sound input card and a microphone. **4**
   (d) Outline how you would go about transferring music from an audio cassette tape recording to audio CD (on CD-R media) using multimedia hardware and software. You should give details of all data formats used. **3**

7. A computer based learning package about driving a car will contain moving images. These could either be video or an animated sequence. The software used limits the size of the moving images to 5 cm square.
   (a) Describe the characteristics of each of these forms of moving image representation in terms of their storage requirements, data representation and data input methods. **5**
   (b) What advantages could there be for the user of the training package if an animated sequence were used instead of video? **2**
   (c) Computer training packages like this can be enhanced by creating 3 dimensional effects. Describe any **one** technique which can produce 3D effects on a computer system. **3**

[END OF QUESTION PAPER]

2000 HIGHER

X017/301

NATIONAL
QUALIFICATIONS
2000

FRIDAY, 9 JUNE
9.00 AM – 11.30 AM

COMPUTING
HIGHER

Attempt **all** questions in Section I.

Attempt **four** questions in Section II

    Question 1 and Question 2
    and **either** Question 3 **or** Question 4
    and **either** Question 5 **or** Question 6

Attempt **one** Sub-Section of Section III. In this Section there are four Sub-Sections, one for each of the Optional Units.

    Computer Programming   —Page nine
    Artificial Intelligence   —Page twelve
    Computer Networking   —Page fifteen
    Multimedia Technology   —Page seventeen

For the Optional Unit chosen, attempt

    Question 1 and Question 2
    and **either** Question 3 **or** Question 4.

Read all questions carefully.

Write your answers in the two answer books provided. One answer book should be used for Sections I and II and the second answer book **must** be used for Section III.

Do not write on the question paper.

Write as neatly as possible.

SECTION I

Attempt all questions in this section

Marks

1. Program design should aim to produce software that is:
   - *reliable*
   - *maintainable*
   - *fit for purpose.*

   (a) State what is meant by **each** of the above terms.   3

   (b) State **one** difference between a problem description and a specification.   1

2. A program converts student marks to grades that are in the range A to E. Each mark is input from the keyboard and must be in the range 0 to 120. If the mark is outside the range, the user is prompted to re-enter the mark.

   (a) Identify **two** data items required in this program and state their data types.   2

   (b) Name **two** software development tools which would be used in implementing this program, and describe the purpose of each.   3

   (c) Which **one** of the following algorithms would be required in this program?
   - (i) Counting occurrences
   - (ii) Linear search
   - (iii) Input validation
   - (iv) Finding minimum   1

3. The first stage in any software development project is *analysis*.

   (a) State the purpose of the *analysis* stage of the software development process.   1

   (b) Describe **two** techniques used by software development staff at the *analysis* stage.   2

4. The image in Figure 1 has been created using a graphics package.

   Figure 1

   Describe **two** ways in which this image could be represented in memory.   4

SECTION I (continued)

Marks

5. Processor clock speed is one factor which affects system performance. Name **one** other factor and describe how it affects system performance. **2**

6. A school pupil loads a file into a workstation from a fileserver. Describe **two** operating system functions needed in order to complete this process. **2**

7. (*a*) What is the purpose of the *control unit* in a CPU? **1**

(*b*) Describe the purpose of **two** signals found on the control bus. **2**

(*c*) State the purpose of registers in a microprocessor. **1**

8. Module libraries are important tools in software development. Describe **two** items of information you would expect to find about a module in a module library's documentation. **2**

9. An advertisement for an application package states that a scripting language is one of its features.

(*a*) Describe **two** characteristics of a scripting language. **2**

(*b*) Give an example of how a scripting language could be used in an application package. **1**

(30)

[Turn over

[END OF SECTION I]

SECTION II

Attempt FOUR questions in this section

Question 1 and Question 2
and <u>either</u> Question 3 <u>or</u> Question 4
and <u>either</u> Question 5 <u>or</u> Question 6

Marks

1. An estate agent has created an on-line database of local properties for sale. Customers are able to browse through the records and print out the records of individual properties. An example is shown in Figure 2.

Figure 2

(a) Each image in the picture field measures 3 inches by 1·5 inches. The image is a grey scale graphic with 256 levels of grey and a resolution of 1200 dots per inch (dpi).

(i) Calculate the storage requirements for **one** photograph. Show your working.

(ii) The database currently holds details of 110 properties. Identify a suitable storage device for the database file that the customers use. Justify your answer.

3

(b) The photographs were scanned using a 1200 dpi, 24 bit colour scanner.

(i) Explain the term "24 bit colour".

(ii) Explain why 1200 dpi may not be the best resolution for this image. In your answer you should make reference to any output device which might be used.

3

(c) The information described above could also have been stored using a different class of application package.

(i) Select a suitable class of application package, other than a database, and describe how the information would have been stored using this class of package.

(ii) Identify **one** advantage and **one** disadvantage of using your chosen class of package rather than a database.

4

Marks

SECTION II (continued)

2. You are the IT manager in a college. The college Principal wishes to invest in a system that tracks student attainment in course examinations.

   Figure 3 below is an extract of the operational requirements of the student tracking system.

   > **Student Tracking**
   > **Operational Requirements**
   >
   > The system should provide:
   > - multi-level access
   > - creation of student details
   > - updating of student details
   > - printing of personalised reports for students
   > - student results summary

   Figure 3

   You recommend the use of a general purpose application package.

   (a) Give **two** advantages of using a general purpose application package rather than designing a special purpose program. **2**

   (b) The application package supports the creation of *macros*.
   - (i) What is meant by the term *macro*?
   - (ii) Choose **one** of the operational requirements in Figure 3. Describe how a macro could be used to implement this operational requirement. **3**

   (c) The college Principal is worried about the maintenance of the student tracking system. Identify **two** maintenance activities and, for each activity, explain why it may be necessary. **3**

   (d) Explain how the use of multi-level access will assist the college in complying with any legal requirements regarding the handling of personal data. **2**

   [Turn over

Marks

SECTION II (continued)

Attempt either Question 3 or Question 4

3. *Event driven* programming languages differ from *declarative* languages and more traditional *procedural* languages in the way programs are executed.

   (a) Describe how programs are executed in each of these three types of language.   3

   (b) Describe a type of problem in software development where an event driven language would be necessary. Give **two** reasons to justify your choice.   2

   (c) When using an event driven program, input from the keyboard or mouse is by serial data transmission.

   Explain what is meant by *serial data transmission*, and describe how it differs from *parallel data transmission*.   3

   (d) Serial to parallel data conversion is one function carried out by a serial interface. Describe **two** other tasks carried out by an interface.   2

4. All modern computers are *stored program* machines made from two-state devices.

   (a) Explain what is meant by the *stored program* concept.   1

   (b) Digital computers use binary codes to represent data. Give **two** reasons why computers are based on the binary number system.   2

   (c) Describe the main stages of the *fetch-execute* cycle in a stored program computer.   2

   (d) Developments in computer design have included increases in the size of both address and data buses. Describe the implications of both of these increases for the processing capabilities of computer systems.   2

   (e) Explain how the size of the data and address buses could affect a software developer's choice of Human Computer Interface (HCI) for a program.   3

Marks

SECTION II (continued)

Attempt either Question 5 or Question 6

5. Clydeside Local Council is commissioning a computerised timetabling package to be developed for use in all of its schools. This large scale project will require best practice in software development.

    (a) (i) Explain why it is important to construct test data before coding begins.

    (ii) List the categories of test data that should be prepared to test the package. **3**

    (b) The package is coded using a compiled high level language.

    (i) Explain how the use of *local variables* and *parameter passing* can aid the portability of software.

    (ii) Why is it important that the software produced should be portable? **3**

    (c) State **two** reasons why modular programming is common practice when a team of programmers is working on a large program. **2**

    (d) The size of the final program and associated files is 17 Megabytes. None of the individual files is larger than 1·2 Megabytes. State **one** advantage and **one** disadvantage of distributing the package on each of the following:

    (i) a set of floppy discs;

    (ii) a CD ROM. **2**

[Turn over

SECTION II (continued)

6. GlobalRead sells books on the Internet. Customers send a list of International Standard Book Numbers (ISBN) via a Web page. The list is processed on GlobalRead's computer. A 5% discount is given on an order if 3 or more of the books ordered cost over £25 each, or if the total cost of the order is more than £250.

   A typical ISBN is 0201549794

   (a) Explain why the ISBN should be stored as a string. **1**

   (b) Part of the processing of an order is described in the structure diagram shown in Figure 4.

   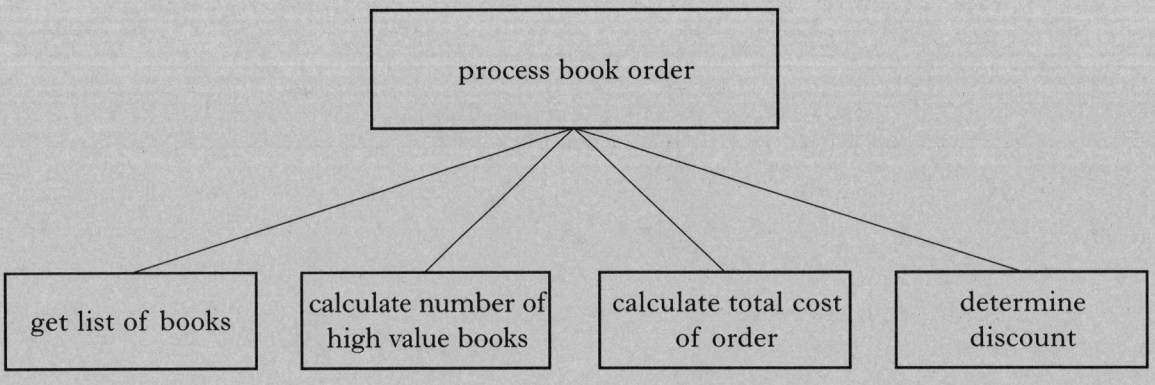

   Figure 4

   For each of the two modules, *calculate total cost of order* and *determine discount*, identify the parameters that would be needed. For each parameter, state its data type, and whether it would be passed *by reference* or *by value*. **4**

   (c) The module *determine discount* requires a complex condition. Give this condition in pseudocode or in the syntax of a computer language you know. **2**

   (d) What iteration control structure should be used in the module *get list of books*? Give **one** reason. **1**

   (e) It is inefficient of processor time to have two separate modules *calculate number of high value books* and *calculate total cost of order*. Explain why this is inefficient. **2**

[END OF SECTION II]

You must write your answers for section III in the second answer book provided.

SECTION III—Computer Programming

Attempt Question 1 and Question 2 and either Question 3 or Question 4

Marks

1. In developing software, a programmer uses a variety of development tools.

   (a) **Two** common development tools are *editors* and *debuggers*. Describe **each** of these tools. Your answer should refer to the following:

   (i) purpose of the tool;

   (ii) stage(s) of software development that makes use of the tool.   **3**

   (b) Describe **two** facilities which you would expect to find in a *programming text editor* which you would not expect to find in a general purpose text editor or word processing package.   **2**

   (c) Debugging can be carried out entirely manually or it can be assisted by a development environment.

   (i) Describe **one** manual method of debugging.

   (ii) Describe **two** ways in which a development environment can provide assistance with debugging.   **3**

   (d) Two forms of translators are *interpreters* and *compilers*.

   (i) Explain how the use of an interpreter can reduce overall development time.

   (ii) Describe how error reporting is handled by a compiler.   **2**

2. Internal searching and sorting algorithms make use of list data structures. Two special forms of list data structures are *queues* and *stacks*.

   (a) Describe the differences in operation of a queue and a stack. You may use labelled diagrams to illustrate your answer.   **3**

   (b) Describe in pseudocode, or in another suitable form, **one** of the main operations of a stack.   **3**

   (c) (i) Describe how a binary search algorithm works.

   (ii) Construct a list of data. Use the list to demonstrate the improved efficiency of binary search compared to linear search in the use of processor time.   **4**

[Turn over

SECTION III—Computer Programming (continued)

Attempt either Question 3 or Question 4

3. Figure 5(a) shows the initial arrangement of tiles in a puzzle. Tile "11" could be moved down into the space, **or** tile "7" could be moved to the left into the space. To solve the puzzle, a player has to move the tiles into the goal arrangement shown in Figure 5(b).

A software developer is writing a program which will allow this game to be played on a computer.

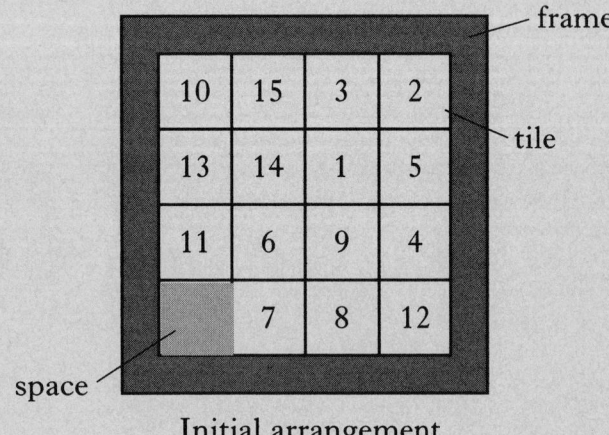

Initial arrangement
Figure 5(a)

Goal arrangement
Figure 5(b)

(a) Name a high level language (HLL) with which you are familiar. Describe how this HLL could represent the arrangement of the tiles using **one** of the following data structures:
- a two-dimensional array
- a record
- one-dimensional arrays in parallel.

3

(b) A factor in implementing one of the data structures in (a) is the *maintainability* of the program code.

Describe **three** characteristics of an implementation that would aid maintenance. Show how these characteristics would be implemented in the HLL that you have chosen in (a).

3

(c) Choose **two** data structures from (a). For each data structure, describe in pseudocode or program code how the initial arrangement of the square frame in Figure 5(a) is set up.

4

SECTION III—Computer Programming (continued)

4. A program has been written to process a sequential file of text. The program detects words within the text file and stores each word in a two-dimensional array. A search word is entered and the program reports the line number(s) within the original text file which include(s) the search word and the number of times that this search word occurs.

   Figure 6(a) shows the contents of the text file and Figure 6(b) shows the corresponding contents of the two-dimensional array.

   > Let us not forget the wisdom
   > Of knowledge being something
   > You acquire after you need it.

   Figure 6(a) File of text

Let	us	not	forget	the	wisdom
Of	knowledge	being	something		
You	acquire	after	you	need	it

   Figure 6(b) Two-dimensional array

   (a) How does the program detect the end of a word in the text file? **1**

   (b) Describe how finding the number of occurrences of a given search word in the two-dimensional array could be carried out. You may use pseudocode or program code to illustrate your answer. **4**

   (c) This method of storage of words is not efficient, since array elements are unused when lines have few words. Describe an alternative method of storing words in memory which makes more efficient use of memory. Your method must include a way of identifying the end of a line. **2**

   (d) One method of ensuring that the program is robust is to carry out *systematic* and *comprehensive* testing.
       (i) Explain what is meant by **each** of the above terms.
       (ii) Describe how each of the above can affect the *robustness* of a program. **3**

[Turn over

You must write your answers for section III in the second answer book provided.

SECTION III—Artificial Intelligence

Attempt Question 1 and Question 2 and either Question 3 or Question 4

Marks

1. (a) (i) What is the function of an expert system?
   (ii) Why is it important for an expert system to justify its reasoning?   **3**

   (b) A primary school teacher wants to have an expert system about dinosaurs for her pupils to use in projects.

   Here is some information which she would like to have included in the system.

   "Dinosaurs ate either meat or plants. The following are examples of dinosaurs and the food they ate. Eustreptospondylus dinosaurs ate meat, they had sharp teeth and powerful jaws. Tyrannosaurus Rex was a meat eater and had powerful jaws. Multaburrasaurus had a beak-like mouth and ate plants."

   Design rules to represent this information, using a form with which you are familiar.   **3**

   (c) Knowledge bases can be searched using either *depth first* or *breadth first* search algorithms.
   (i) Describe what is meant by **each** of these search methods. You may use diagrams to illustrate your answer.
   (ii) Give **one** advantage and **one** disadvantage of using depth first searching rather than breadth first searching.   **4**

SECTION III—Artificial Intelligence (continued)

2. The following knowledge base has been designed to help parents decide if children can view a particular film on cable TV.

   ```
   1.  persons_age (kirsten 12)        means that kirsten is 12 years old
   2.  persons_age (peter 16)          etc
   3.  persons_age (zoe 18)
   4.  persons_age (katie 6)
   5.  persons_age (euan 9)
   6.  film (starjourney U)            means that film starjourney is category U
   7.  film (hungariantale 15)         etc
   8.  film (argojason U)
   9.  film (theseeker 12)
   10. film (catch 18)
   11. can_see (X,Y) if film (Y Z)     means that person X can see film Y if film Y is category Z
       and persons_age (X W)           and person X is W years old
       and (W >= Z)                    and W is greater than or equal to Z
   ```

   (a) (i) What would be the result from the following query?

   ?can_see (katie hungariantale)

   (ii) Explain how the system would evaluate the query

   ?can_see (kirsten theseeker) **4**

   (b) The program should be able to deal with the query

   ?can_see (katie starjourney)

   (i) Why would this query not be solved correctly?

   (ii) Describe **two** ways in which the knowledge base could be amended to allow the query to be solved. **3**

   (c) The knowledge base has to be extended so that searches can be carried out to find films by category, eg films that feature animals.

   (i) Design a rule which will indicate that the film "theseeker" features animals.

   (ii) Design a rule "is_suggested_for (P Q R)" which will identify films that child Q can see and that feature category R. **3**

[Turn over

SECTION III—Artificial Intelligence (continued)

Answer either Question 3 or Question 4

3. A company that produces tins of wrapped sweets wishes to use recycled tins. The company is investigating the use of an intelligent robot to examine tins to make sure they are fit for re-use. Slightly deformed tins may be re-used. Badly damaged tins should be rejected. See Figure 7.

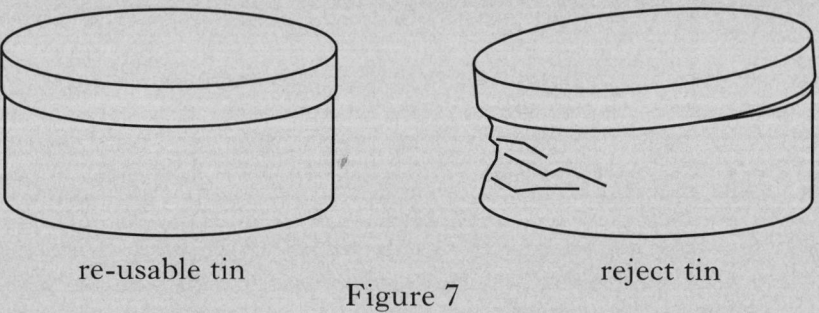

re-usable tin   reject tin

Figure 7

To develop this system, several areas of artificial intelligence must be considered. Two such areas are *computer vision* and *pattern recognition*.

(a) How would pattern recognition be used to identify a re-usable tin?   **2**

(b) What problems could arise when computer vision is used to select re-usable tins?   **2**

(c) (i) What is meant by the term *heuristics*?

    (ii) How could heuristics be used in identifying which tins to re-use?

    (iii) Describe **one** other situation in which heuristics could be used.   **4**

(d) Changes in the way computers process data have made such robots possible. Explain **one** method of processing data in this situation. You may use a diagram to illustrate your answer.   **2**

4. (a) Identify the main achievement in the field of artificial intelligence in each of these periods:

    (i) 1950 to mid 1960s;

    (ii) mid 1960s to mid 1970s;

    (iii) late 1970s onwards.   **3**

(b) In the early days of artificial intelligence the question "can machines think?" was raised. Describe the test which was proposed to determine whether a computer could "think".   **2**

(c) (i) What is the aim of *natural language processing*?

    (ii) Describe **one** application of natural language processing.

    (iii) Describe **two** problems which might occur in the operation of your chosen application.   **5**

You must write your answers for section III in the second answer book provided.

SECTION III—Computer Networking

Attempt Question 1 and Question 2 and either Question 3 or Question 4

Marks

1. Tannford High School has a bus network linking computers in the Computing department. The school wishes to extend the network to include existing computers in all other departments and in the school office.

    (a) Describe **two** benefits that this extension of the network could provide for teachers in the school. **2**

    (b) The ICT Co-ordinator suggests that a star topology would be more appropriate than a bus topology. State **one** reason in favour of retaining the bus topology, and **one** reason in favour of the star topology. **2**

    (c) Teaching staff want to be able to access the World Wide Web from any computer in the school.

    　(i) What additional piece of hardware would be required to link the school LAN to the Internet?

    　(ii) Why would this be required? **2**

    (d) A school web site is to be set up.

    　(i) Distinguish between HTTP and HTML.

    　(ii) Suggest a full URL for the school's home page, and describe the purpose of each part of the URL. **4**

2. ScotDTP is a small company of 4 graphic designers who produce advertising and leaflets using computer hardware and software. At present they operate using a small LAN that links 6 computers and 2 printers in the company's town centre office. To reduce costs ScotDTP has decided that the graphic designers should work from home and that the office should be closed. The graphic designers will communicate by connecting their computers to a WAN.

    (a) Apart from the greater distances between computers in a typical WAN, describe **two** other differences between a WAN and a LAN. **2**

    (b) Describe **two** disadvantages (**one** technical and **one** social) of the decision that the graphic designers should work from home, and suggest how these could be overcome. **4**

    (c) A DTP project requires a photograph of a wildebeest, which is also called a gnu.

    　(i) What type of software is required to access the World Wide Web (WWW)?

    　(ii) Describe how such a photograph could be found and downloaded from the WWW.

    　(iii) What are the legal implications of downloading a photograph from the WWW? **4**

[Turn over

Marks

SECTION III—Computer Networking (continued)

Answer either Question 3 or Question 4

3. Duncan and Sharon Smith each have a computer in their rooms at home. Their mum and dad have a computer in the study. Sharon suggests that they should network their computers.

   (a) The network could be a *peer-to-peer* network, or a *client-server* network.
   - (i) Describe clearly **two** main differences between peer-to-peer and client-server networks.
   - (ii) Give **two** reasons why a peer-to-peer network would be more suitable for the Smith family.
   - (iii) Name a suitable network operating system for peer-to-peer networking.   5

   (b) The Smith family decides to have cabling installed for the network.
   - (i) State **two** of the main options available for the network cabling. State, giving **one** reason, which of these you would recommend.
   - (ii) What bandwidth can they expect from this network?
   - (iii) The Smiths' network is likely to use a protocol called CSMA/CD. Explain clearly what this term means.   5

4. (a) The US Defence internetwork (ARPANET) gave rise to the modern Internet.
   - (i) What is an "internetwork"?
   - (ii) Describe **two** factors which have led to the recent rapid growth of ARPANET into the "Internet".   3

   (b) The Internet uses *packet-switching* to transfer data from computer to computer, using a protocol family called TCP/IP.
   - (i) What does TCP/IP mean?
   - (ii) What is meant by the term *packet-switching*?
   - (iii) Describe the roles of the *TCP* and *IP* layers when a large file is transferred between two computers on an internetwork.   5

   (c) The OSI model of network communication describes 7 layers or levels.
   - (i) At which level does TCP operate?
   - (ii) At which level does IP operate?   2

You must write your answers for section III in the second answer book provided.

SECTION III—Multimedia Technology

Attempt Question 1 and Question 2 and either Question 3 or Question 4

Marks

1. Training programs often take the form of a multimedia presentation comprising text, graphics and sound.

    (a) Describe **two** different types of multimedia authoring software which would allow such a presentation to be *created*.

    State **one** advantage and **one** disadvantage of each. **3**

    (b) (i) Why is data compression useful in multimedia presentations?

    (ii) Describe **one** data compression technique used for audio data. **3**

    (c) Many graphics file formats exist. This allows portability of files and code among different applications and different hardware. Examples of file formats include PCX, TIFF, BMP, EPS, PICT, GIF, JPEG.

    Identify **two** graphics file formats and explain how data is stored in each of them. **4**

2. A small publishing company relies on materials from many sources to produce both paper based and software products. OCR software is often used for text input.

    (a) Describe how OCR software operates to input text into a DTP application. **2**

    (b) Describe **two** differences in the way DTP packages and hypermedia authoring packages are used. **2**

    (c) Describe **three** techniques that may be applied using a bit-mapped graphics package that could not be applied using a vector graphics package. **3**

    (d) Explain why a hypermedia system would be more useful for computer based training than an electronic "book" created and viewed with a word processing package. **3**

[Turn over

SECTION III—Multimedia Technology (continued)

Answer either Question 3 or Question 4

3. A modern multimedia computer has the following hardware: 4 Gb hard disk, 32Mb RAM, 16 speed CD ROM, CPU at 500MHz, audio card, speakers, video card and 15" colour monitor. Additional hardware is required if professional presentations are to be created using this computer.

   (a) Describe in technical detail how video hardware technology for capture, compression and display has developed and enhanced multimedia presentation.

   (b) As well as hardware, multimedia devices require the installation of system extensions to the basic system *software*. With reference to Figure 8 below, describe the purpose of each of the layers within the multimedia environment.

   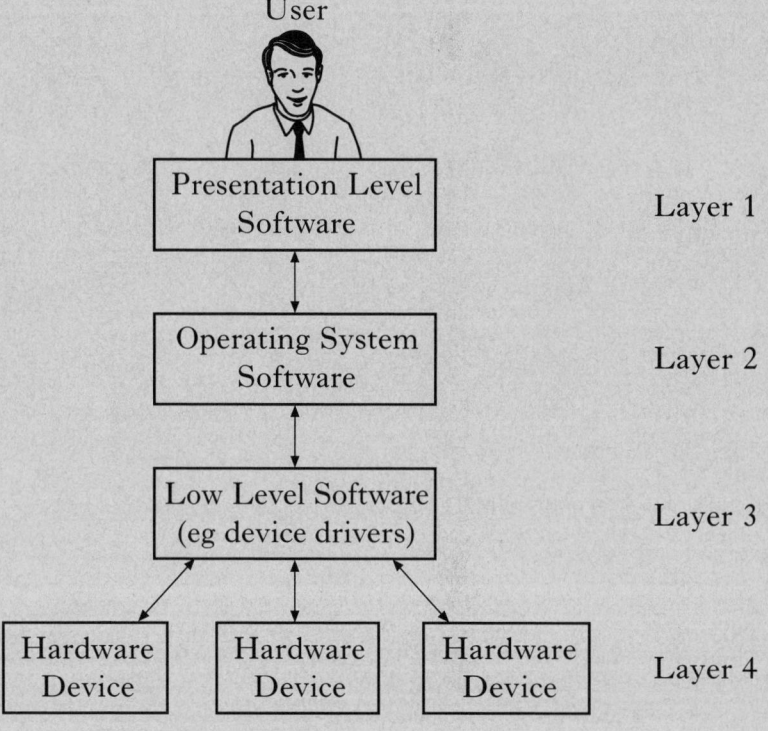

   Figure 8

   (c) State **two** reasons why the issue of copyright is important when creating multimedia presentations.

SECTION III—Multimedia Technology (continued)

4. Figure 9 illustrates a standard studio set up where a MIDI keyboard sends data to be recorded directly into a computer software sequencer.

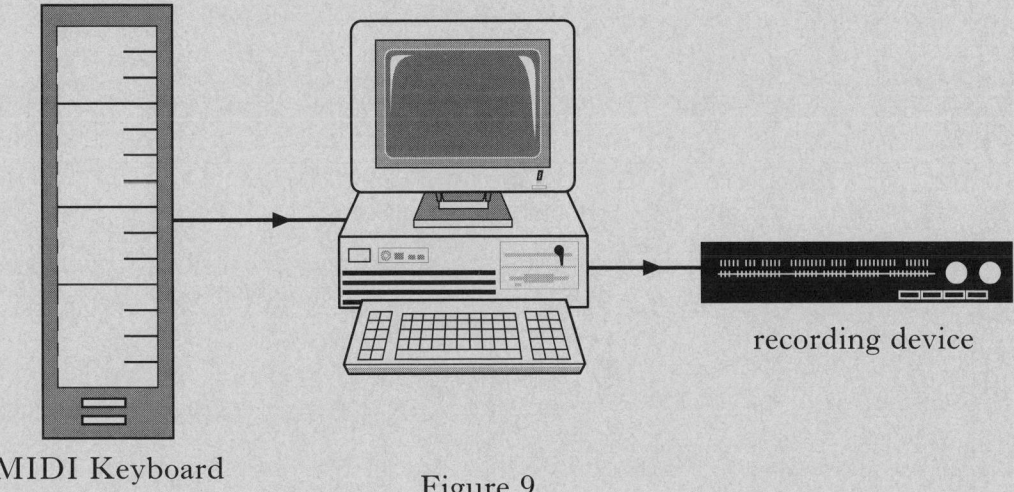

MIDI Keyboard   Figure 9   recording device

(a) Name **three** pieces of information that could be contained in a single MIDI message. **3**

(b) (i) Software sequencers have a choice of facilities for viewing data prior to editing. Explain why the scope for editing is more flexible with sequenced data.

(ii) Name **two** editing operations that could be performed on the data. **3**

(c) Many sound cards are capable of both *frequency modulation* and *wave table synthesis*. Describe **each** of these processes. **4**

[END OF SECTION III]

[END OF QUESTION PAPER]

[BLANK PAGE]

2001 HIGHER

X017/301

| NATIONAL QUALIFICATIONS 2001 | TUESDAY, 5 JUNE 1.00 PM – 3.30 PM | COMPUTING HIGHER |

Attempt **all** questions in Section I.

Attempt **four** questions in Section II

    Question 13 and Question 14
    and **either** Question 15 **or** Question 16
    and **either** Question 17 **or** Question 18

Attempt **one** sub-section of Section III.

Part A	Artificial Intelligence	Page 12	Questions 19 to 22
Part B	Computer Networking	Page 15	Questions 23 to 26
Part C	Computer Programming	Page 18	Questions 27 to 30
Part D	Multimedia Technology	Page 22	Questions 31 to 34

For the sub-section chosen, attempt **three** questions.

The **first two** questions and **either** the third question **or** the fourth question.

Read all questions carefully.

Do not write on the question paper.

Write as neatly as possible.

SECTION I

Attempt all questions in this section

Marks

1. A desktop computer is connected to a local-area network.

   (a) Name and draw a labelled diagram of **one** network topology which could be used for the local-area network. 1

   (b) What specific hardware must be present in a computer in order for it to be connected to this network? 1

2. Buffers and spoolers can be used to increase system performance.

   (a) Describe how a buffer will increase system performance. 1

   (b) Describe **one** situation in which a spooler would be used in preference to a buffer. 1

3. Describe **two** different methods you could use to find out whether a graphic was created using a bit-mapped graphics package or a vector graphics package. 2

4. A scanned image measures 3 inches by 4 inches. It was scanned at 600 dpi in 256 colours.

   (a) Calculate the storage requirements for the scanned image in megabytes. Show all your working. 2

   (b) Name **one** storage device which could be used to store the image and give **one** reason for your choice. 2

5. (a) In computer systems, integers are stored using *two's complement representation*. What would be the range of integers which could be stored in **one** byte if two's complement representation was used? 1

   (b) In computer systems, large numbers are stored using *floating point representation*. State the effect of **increasing** the number of bits used to store:
      (i) the mantissa;
      (ii) the exponent. 2

6. Give **one** reason why a computer is often described as a "two-state machine". 1

7. How is memory organised so that data can be stored and retrieved by the processor? 1

SECTION I (continued)

Marks

8. A list of medals won at the Olympic Games is stored in a computer. For each medal, details of the event, name and country of the winner are stored. A program was designed to work out how many medals overall each country won.

   (a) Which **one** of the following algorithms would be needed in this program?
      (i) Finding maximum
      (ii) Finding minimum
      (iii) Counting occurrences
      (iv) Linear search 1

   (b) Name **two** guides which should be produced during the documentation stage of the software development process. 1

   (c) Give **one** advantage to the software house of distributing these guides on CD ROM. 1

9. The first two stages of the software development process are *analysis* and *design*.

   (a) State the purpose of each of these stages. 2

   (b) What is meant by the term *iterative* during the software development process? 1

10. (a) Give **one** reason why it is important for programmers to ensure that their programs are readable. 1

    (b) Describe **two** different techniques used by programmers to ensure that their programs are readable. 2

11. Describe the purpose of each of the following in a software development environment:
    (i) editor;
    (ii) translator;
    (iii) error tracing tool. 3

12. (a) Some software development environments support *local variables* as well as *global variables*.
       (i) State what is meant by a "local variable".
       (ii) Describe how the use of local variables assists with modularity. 2

    (b) State **one** method of storing a list of 100 names input from a keyboard within a program. 1

    (30)

[*END OF SECTION I*]

SECTION II

Attempt FOUR questions in this section   Marks

Question 13 and Question 14
and either Question 15 or Question 16
and either Question 17 or Question 18

13. A small company with 200 customers wants to purchase new computers. The IT Manager has noticed two adverts in a computer catalogue.

Pegasus ZX	Hercules EN
333 MHz Processor	366 MHz Processor
64 Mb RAM	64 Mb RAM
2 USB Interfaces	Serial and Parallel Interfaces
4 Gb Hard Disk Drive	10 Gb Hard Disk Drive
24 × CD ROM Drive	40 × CD ROM Drive

    (a) (i) Give **two** reasons why *interfaces* are required to connect peripheral devices to the computer.

    (ii) State why there is a need for standardisation of interfaces.

    (iii) In addition to the interface, what addition to the standard operating system will be required so that the CD ROM drive will operate in these computer systems?   4

    (b) The IT Manager believes that the Hercules EN will be the faster computer as it has a 366 MHz processor compared to the 333 MHz Pegasus ZX.

    Suggest **two** reasons why he may be incorrect.   2

    (c) Both systems have 64 Mb of RAM organised as 32-bit words. What is the minimum possible width of the address bus in these systems? Justify your answer.   2

    (d) Since the company may have to store sensitive data about their customers, describe **two** conditions which the company must satisfy in order to protect their customers.   2

SECTION II (continued)

14. A program requires the user to input the name of the country where they live. The program is able to accept any one of 157 different country names.

Here are three possible means of entering this information in a graphical user interface.

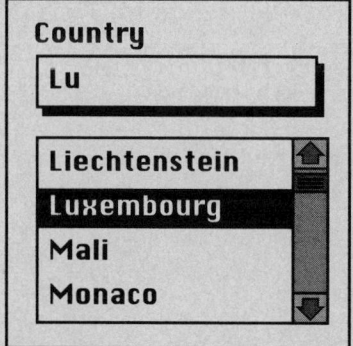

The user types a name into the box.

The user picks one of the names from the scrolling pop-up menu.

The user can type a name or select from the scrollable list. If the user types, the list automatically scrolls to the closest match in the list. The user can still select from the list at any time.

(a) Describe each of these interfaces in terms of:
  - ease of data entry
  - validity of data entry. **3**

(b) If you were the designer of such a program, which **two** questions would you ask to decide which one of these interfaces to specify? **2**

(c) Describe how you could test which one of these interfaces was most suitable for this particular purpose. **2**

(d) This software will have to be maintained when the name of a country changes. How would the change of a country's name affect the maintenance requirement for each of the three interfaces? **3**

[Turn over

SECTION II (continued)

Attempt either Question 15 or Question 16

15. A video firm creates and edits digital videos using their company's computer system.

    (a) Name **three** hardware features that the firm's **computer** must have in order to cope with this task. Give a reason for each of your choices. **3**

    (b) The video company also uses digital cameras.

        (i) Name **two** characteristics which affect the cost of a digital camera.

        (ii) Describe **two** advantages of using a digital camera compared to an ordinary photographic camera. **3**

    (c) A printer has to be used so that the company can print out photographs. State **two** characteristics which this printer should have. Justify your answers. **2**

    (d) The company wishes to create and distribute a searchable electronic catalogue of its best photographs. Describe how this could be done, mentioning any hardware or software required for the purpose. **2**

SECTION II (continued)

16. A programmer has written a program which tests pupils on their knowledge of computer systems. A typical layout is shown below.

The program displays questions which have been stored in a disk file. The pupil selects an answer from a list of answers. The program then checks the answer entered by the pupil and displays a suitable comment. Data on the pupil's performance is saved to disk.

The difficulty of the questions can be altered by using a dialog box which appears when a menu option is selected from a pull down menu. Default settings are set up when the program loads.

(a) Describe **two** features of an event driven programming language which would make it particularly suitable for writing such a program. **2**

(b) Another programmer suggests that a procedural language could be used to write this program.

How do procedural languages differ from event driven languages? **2**

(c) The program uses calls to operating system functions while it is running.

Describe **two** functions of an operating system which the finished program described here would need to use. **2**

(d) The program could also be created in some classes of applications package. Describe **two** advantages and **two** difficulties of using an applications package rather than a programming language to produce this program.

You do not have to describe in detail how to create the program in an applications package, but you may illustrate your answer with examples, referring to one or more class of package. **4**

[Turn over

SECTION II (continued)

Attempt either Question 17 or Question 18

17. A program deals with the results of 10 tests taken by a computing student. The results are given as percentages.

    (a) State a *complex condition* which would be needed in an input validation procedure for the data. **1**

    (b) The program contains a number of procedures and functions.
    Describe **two** advantages of using parameter passing rather than global variables to allow data flow in the program. **2**

    (c) The programmer could use ten *variables* or a *one-dimensional array* to represent the results in the program.
    Compare these strategies in terms of:
    (i) use of storage space;
    (ii) readability of the program;
    (iii) parameter passing. **3**

    (d) When the program is written using a one-dimensional array, the data is passed to procedures as a parameter. Describe **two** differences between passing the list of results as a parameter *by reference* and *by value*. **4**

Marks

SECTION II (continued)

18. A program is being written that will search for a value in a list of integers. The program will report whether the value has been found together with the position of the first occurrence of the value in the list of integers. An appropriate error message will be reported if the value is not present in the list of integers.

Below is a level 1 algorithm for this program.

Steps of Level 1 Algorithm
1. get search item
2. search list of numbers for search item
3. report findings

(a) For step 2 in the algorithm above:
  (i) state the parameters required and their data types;
  (ii) for each parameter, state the parameter passing mechanism. **3**

(b) Step 2 needs to make use of a *complex condition* to control a conditional loop. Describe the complex condition needed in step 2. **1**

(c) The programmer has access to a module library which contains a suitable coded search algorithm to be used for step 2. Give **two** advantages, apart from saving time, of using the module library rather than coding it from scratch. **2**

(d) The programmer has decided to modify this algorithm to store the positions of **all** of the occurrences of the search item in the list of integers.
  (i) What change will be required in the loop in step 2?
  (ii) What additional data items will be required to store all of the positions where the search item is found? **4**

[*END OF SECTION II*]

[**Turn over**

[BLANK PAGE]

SECTION III

Attempt ONE sub-section of Section III

Part A	Artificial Intelligence	Page 12	Questions 19 to 22
Part B	Computer Networking	Page 15	Questions 23 to 26
Part C	Computer Programming	Page 18	Questions 27 to 30
Part D	Multimedia Technology	Page 22	Questions 31 to 34

For the sub-section chosen, attempt three questions

the <u>first two</u> questions and <u>either</u> the third question <u>or</u> the fourth question.

[Turn over

SECTION III

Part A—Artificial Intelligence

**Attempt Question 19 and Question 20
and either Question 21 or Question 22**

19. A software company has been contracted to develop an expert system to advise sailors on weather forecasting.

    (a) (i) What stages in the development process should take place before implementation of the software?

    (ii) Describe clearly the roles of the knowledge engineer and domain experts in these stages. **3**

    (b) (i) The company decides to use an expert system shell to implement the software. Clearly explain the difference between an *expert system* and an *expert system shell*.

    (ii) State **one** advantage and **one** disadvantage of using an expert system shell for the development compared with coding the expert system in a declarative language. **3**

    (c) The following information is to be included in the expert system.

    > "Wind speed is very likely to increase if the wind direction is southerly and the air pressure is falling. Wind speed may increase if the wind direction is northerly and the air pressure is falling."

    (i) Design rules which could represent this information in a form with which you are familiar.

    (ii) Explain how your rules distinguish between "very likely" and "may".

    (iii) Describe **one** legal implication of this expert system being made available commercially. **4**

SECTION III

Part A—Artificial Intelligence (continued)

20. The following knowledge base holds information about some British mountains.

    ```
    1. mountain (snowdon,wales,3560)        Snowdon is a mountain in Wales which is 3560ft high
    2. mountain (scafell,england,3162)      etc
    3. mountain (ben_nevis,scotland,4406)
    4. mountain (ben_lomond,scotland,3192)
    5. mountain (hart_fell,scotland,2400)
    6. munro (X) if                          A Munro is a mountain in Scotland over 3000ft high
       mountain (X,scotland,H)   and
       H>3000
    ```

    (a) (i) What would be the result of the following query?

    ?mountain (ben_nevis,X,Y)

    (ii) Write a query which would list all the mountains in Scotland. **2**

    (b) Assuming a depth-first search is used, explain how the program would find a solution to the following query.

    ?munro (ben_nevis) **2**

    (c) A "furth" is a mountain over 3000ft high which is not in Scotland. Design a rule to represent this information. **2**

    (d) An alternative representation of the facts could be in the form:

    ```
    height(snowdon,3560)
    height(scafell,3162)
    height(ben_nevis,4406)
    height(ben_lomond,3192)
    height(hart_fell,2400)

    country(snowdon,wales)
    country(scafell,england)
    country(ben_nevis,scotland)
    country(ben_lomond,scotland)
    country(hart_fell,scotland)
    ```

    (i) Design a "munro" rule for use with this representation.

    (ii) The completed knowledge base will contain information about **all** British mountains. Explain a disadvantage of this second representation once the knowledge base is in operation. **4**

[Turn over

SECTION III

Part A—Artificial Intelligence (continued)

Attempt either Question 21 or Question 22

21. Some of the earliest artificial intelligence research related to rule-based systems for playing strategic games such as chess which have a large number of game positions and possible moves.

    (a) Describe **two** difficulties in developing a rule-based system for playing chess. **2**

    (b) Name **two** hardware developments which allow modern chess playing systems to be much more successful than those of the 1960s and describe how the developments make this possible. **2**

    (c) Explain the purpose of *heuristics* in such rule-based systems. **1**

    (d) It could be argued that a rule-based system is not really intelligent. Describe a feature of a system which, if implemented, would justify the system being considered intelligent. **2**

    (e) A world chess champion has been beaten by a chess playing computer.

    (i) Describe another area of human ability where computer programs appear to show intelligence.

    (ii) "There are some areas of human ability where a computer program could never out-perform a human." Do you agree? Justify your answer. **3**

22. One area of successful artificial intelligence research is the development of artificial neural networks.

    (a) (i) State **one** limitation of an artificial neural network in comparison to a human brain.

    (ii) Describe how a neural network can be trained to display intelligent behaviour.

    (iii) Name an example of a successful use of neural networks in the "real world".

    (iv) State **one** objection to the use of neural networks in safety-critical applications. **5**

    (b) Another area of artificial intelligence research is the development of computer vision.

    (i) Describe **two** hardware developments that have contributed to the development of this area of artificial intelligence.

    (ii) Describe how computer vision can increase the effectiveness of industrial robots.

    (iii) Describe **one** other feature which would allow an industrial robot to be described as intelligent. **5**

[END OF SECTION III PART A]

SECTION III

Part B—Computer Networking

**Attempt Question 23 and Question 24
and either Question 25 or Question 26**

Marks

23. A newspaper journalist has a laptop computer and a digital camera. She can submit her stories and pictures from anywhere in the world by transferring data to the server in the central office.

    (a) List the hardware and software required to manage the communication between the laptop and the server computer and state the purpose of each item. **3**

    (b) (i) Explain the need for *communications protocols* in this situation.

      (ii) State **two** parameters which a protocol might define. **2**

    (c) (i) Explain the need for security in this situation.

      (ii) Describe **two** security measures which could be taken. **3**

    (d) In the central office, appropriate departments carry out further processing, such as text processing and digital image enhancement, on the journalist's files. These departments access the files from the server using the office local-area network (LAN).

      Describe **two** differences between the characteristics of the data communication on the office LAN compared to the journalist's original data transfer. **2**

24. A large company has a Glasgow office and an Edinburgh office which both have local-area networks (LANs) of desktop computers.

    The company want to connect the two LANs so that any computer on the Edinburgh LAN can access data which is stored on a server on the Glasgow LAN.

    The TCP/IP protocol stack will be used on all computers.

    (a) (i) State the hardware necessary to connect the two LANs.

      (ii) What is the name given to a network of this type? **2**

    (b) Describe how the TCP/IP protocols manage the transfer of a file between two computers on this network. **2**

    (c) The two LANs could be connected using a fixed leased line or ISDN. Describe **one** advantage and **one** disadvantage of **each** method. **2**

    (d) The company wants to provide information services by installing a Web server in one office. The information stored on the Web server will be accessed using Internet style software such as browsers.

      (i) Name a protocol which might be used to control the transfer of data from the Web server computer to the Web browser software and describe its purpose.

      (ii) Describe **one** advantage and **one** disadvantage of storing all of the information service data on a single server in one office rather than having two copies, one in each office. **4**

SECTION III

Part B—Computer Networking (continued)

Answer either Question 25 or Question 26

25. A school office has a local-area network of desktop computers. Each office worker has arranged for **one** folder on their local hard disk to be shared so that other workers can copy files out of that folder. This allows workers to transfer files and messages between their computers.

    (a) (i) What name is given to this type of networking?
        (ii) How can each worker ensure that only certain workers can access the shared folder on their computer?
        (iii) How can they ensure that the other workers can only copy out of the folder and not into the folder? **3**

    (b) The school management have decided that it would be better to store all shared files on a central computer so that all office staff can access them from there. This was decided on the grounds of data security and data integrity.
        (i) What name is given to this type of networking?
        (ii) Name **one** additional item of software and **one** additional item of hardware that would be required to implement this new system. **3**

    (c) For the type of network described in part (b):
        (i) explain how this mode of networking provides data security and data integrity;
        (ii) describe an additional service which could be provided by this new networking mode and explain why it could not be provided before. **4**

SECTION III

Part B—Computer Networking (continued)

26. A school pupil wants to obtain information on design notations used in software development as part of a homework exercise. She wants to use the Internet to find suitable information. To do this she must use communications software to connect to her Internet Service Provider.

(a) Describe **two** functions of the communications software, other than dialling the telephone number of the Internet Service Provider. **2**

(b) How can she locate a Web site containing descriptions of design notations used in software development if she does not know its URL? **2**

(c) She finds a Web site which has the facility to download a document on the subject. When she clicks on the link, the following URL appears in the location bar of the browser software.

ftp://softdev.org.uk/design.pdf
   A   B   C

Describe the purpose of the parts of URL labelled A, B and C. **2**

(d) She finds that the file takes too long to download and decides to download it in school the next day as she knows that Web pages download faster at school.

Give **two** reasons why Web pages might download faster at school. **2**

(e) When she tries to download the file, she finds that ftp access has been barred.
  (i) Why might ftp access be barred by the school?
  (ii) What application on the school network has barred ftp access? **2**

[END OF SECTION III PART B]

[Turn over

SECTION III

Part C—Computer Programming

**Attempt Question 27 and Question 28
and either Question 29 or Question 30**

Marks

27. The positive integer 25 can be converted to binary by repeated division as follows.

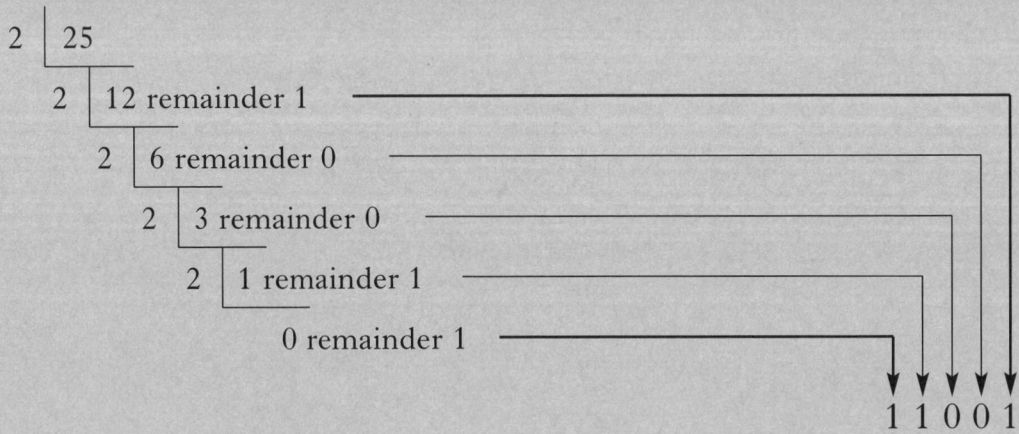

The binary value is obtained by arranging the remainders as shown.

In a program to teach pupils how this process works, the programmer wishes to store the 5 pairs of results (eg 12 and 1, 6 and 0 . . .) in a two-dimensional array.

(a) Describe fully how a *two-dimensional array* could be used to represent the results of each stage in converting a positive integer to binary. **2**

(b) Describe in pseudocode, or otherwise, the process of assigning values to the two-dimensional array. State any limitations of your design. **4**

(c) The same data could be represented using a one-dimensional array.
   (i) Describe how a one-dimensional array could represent this data.
   (ii) Explain how this would make the maintenance of the program more difficult. **4**

SECTION III

Part C—Computer Programming (continued)

Marks

28. A program first reads a list of student names and corresponding examination marks from a text file held on disk. The student names and marks are stored and processed in the computer's memory using parallel one-dimensional arrays.

   (a) A run-time error could occur during the reading of the data from the file in this program.

   (i) State the type of run time error which could occur.

   (ii) Describe how the error could be detected and reported by the program so that the program does not crash. **3**

   (b) Using pseudocode, or another suitable form, describe how data is read from the file and stored in the parallel arrays. **3**

   (c) Student names are to be sorted into ascending alphabetic order.

   (i) What problem arises when sorting the parallel one-dimensional arrays?

   (ii) How would a record structure remove any problems? **2**

   (d) An insert operation finds the correct position in the array at which to store a student name in alphabetic order.

   (i) State **two** conditions that the insert operation needs to test.

   (ii) Using a diagram, show how items are relocated when a new name is inserted. **2**

[Turn over

SECTION III

Part C—Computer Programming (continued)

Answer **either** Question 29 **or** Question 30

29. Compilers have to be able to deal with arithmetic expressions such as

$(9 - 2) * (3 + 4)$

This kind of expression can be transformed into a sequence of symbols thus:

9 2 − 3 4 + *

This is then processed using a *stack data structure* with the following algorithm:

```
loop
  get next symbol
  if symbol is a number then
    push symbol onto stack
  end if
  if symbol is an operator then
    pop the top two items from the stack and carry out the
      operation on these values
    push the result onto the stack
  end if
end loop
```

(a) Using a diagram, show the state of the stack after the symbol "3" has been *pushed* onto it. **2**

(b) Give the upper limit of the size of the stack needed in this case. **1**

(c) Describe, in pseudocode or otherwise, the operation to push a symbol onto the stack. You should mention the types of all data items needed. **3**

(d) A more complex arithmetic expression could cause an error if the size of the stack is set to the value you gave in (a) above.
  (i) What is the name of this error condition?
  (ii) How could the program detect this condition?
  (iii) How could a program deal with this error if it occurs? **4**

Marks

SECTION III

Part C—Computer Programming (continued)

30. A printer buffer uses a *queue data structure* to hold items of data that are to be printed. A queue data structure requires additional data items to support its operations.

   (a) (i) What are the additional data items that are required?

   (ii) When the printer buffer queue is full, what conditions will be true of the additional data items? **2**

   (b) One of these conditions will cause a problem.
   (i) State what the problem is.
   (ii) Outline a solution to this problem. **3**

   (c) Describe how an item is added to the printer buffer queue. You may use labelled diagrams to illustrate your answer. **2**

   (d) Print *server* software stores a data record in a queue, rather than the data itself. The data record contains the username, timestamp and the name of the file in which the print job is stored.

   This allows an administrator to manage the queue, by changing the order of items, removing items from the queue and getting status information.

   Describe, in pseudocode or otherwise, a method of finding the number of items in a print server queue for a given user. **3**

[END OF SECTION III PART C]

[Turn over

SECTION III

Part D—Multimedia Technology

**Attempt Question 31 and Question 32
and either Question 33 or Question 34**

Marks

31. (a) (i) Explain what is meant by the term *authoring tool*.

      (ii) Describe **two** features of an authoring tool which enable the creation of a multimedia application. **4**

(b) Recent developments in hardware and software technologies have contributed to the growth of multimedia. Explain how recent developments in
- optical data storage, and
- sound card technologies

have contributed to this growth. **4**

(c) There are various standard file formats for digitised sound which allow the exchange of sounds between different software packages. Describe the features of **one** such audio file format. **2**

32. Design of the layout is usually undertaken before constructing a multimedia presentation.

(a) State **three** elements of design layout which may be included in the planning of a multimedia presentation. **3**

(b) Icon based and script based software are used to produce the presentation. Explain why a developer may wish to consider the use of a script based development tool within a multimedia authoring package. **2**

(c) The quality of the final presentation may be limited by the display hardware.

      (i) State **three** characteristics of the display hardware which may affect the quality of the final presentation.

      (ii) Describe the role of the video graphics card in overcoming this problem above. **5**

SECTION III

Part D—Multimedia Technology (continued)

Answer **either** Question 33 **or** Question 34

33. A company is producing a tourist information *presentation* comprising various media elements such as video, photographs, text and sound. One of the developers is working from home and communicating electronically with the company headquarters. The developer has scanned an image and saved the file in TIFF format.

   (a) (i) Two different types of scanner are being considered by the company which will allow the developer to scan text and graphics. Apart from cost, describe **two** characteristics which should be used when comparing **two** different types of scanner.

   (ii) Suggest a specification for a scanner for the purpose described. Justify your answer. **4**

   (b) The scanning software by default saves scanned images in TIFF format. Name **one** other format and describe **one** advantage that TIFF has over your chosen format. **1**

   (c) Once the digital images have been received by the company, image processing software is used to carry out further tasks. Describe **three** further image processing tasks that could be carried out. **3**

   (d) Another developer is producing all the text based documents for the presentation. Compare **two** file formats in which the text documents could be sent electronically to the office for inclusion in the presentation. **2**

34. (a) *File compression* is widely used with multimedia elements.
   (i) Name and describe **one** compression technique which can be used with multimedia data.
   (ii) Describe a multimedia situation where this technique may be applied. **3**

   (b) Many graphics file formats are available to the multimedia designer for a variety of purposes. Name and describe the characteristics of **one** file format which comprises bit-mapped data and **one** file format which comprises vector data. **4**

   (c) *Gamma correction* is one feature of graphic manipulation software which adjusts the gamma or mid tones of an image. Describe **three** other features used for manipulation of digitised images in software. **3**

[END OF SECTION III PART D]

[END OF QUESTION PAPER]

[BLANK PAGE]

2002 HIGHER

X017/301

NATIONAL
QUALIFICATIONS
2002

THURSDAY, 6 JUNE
1.00 PM – 3.30 PM

COMPUTING
HIGHER

Attempt **all** questions in Section I.

Attempt **four** questions in Section II

    Question 13 and Question 14
    and **either** Question 15 **or** Question 16
    and **either** Question 17 **or** Question 18

Attempt **one** sub-section of Section III.

Part A	Artificial Intelligence	Page 12	Questions 19 to 22
Part B	Computer Networking	Page 16	Questions 23 to 26
Part C	Computer Programming	Page 19	Questions 27 to 30
Part D	Multimedia Technology	Page 23	Questions 31 to 34

For the sub-section chosen, attempt **three** questions.

The **first two** questions and **either** the third question **or** the fourth question.

Read all questions carefully.

Do not write on the question paper.

Write as neatly as possible.

SECTION I

Attempt all questions in this section

Marks

1. (a) Give **two** reasons why computers use binary numbers to represent and store data. **2**

   (b) Which **one** of the following is the 8-bit two's complement representation of −14?

   (i) 11110001   (ii) 11110010   (iii) 10001110   (iv) 11110011   **1**

2. (a) Describe how *ASCII* is used to represent text. **1**

   (b) Explain what is meant by a *character set*. **1**

3. Modern computers use the *stored program concept*. Explain what is meant by the stored program concept and give **one** advantage of this aspect of computer design. **2**

4. State the purpose of:

   (i) *system software* and

   (ii) *application software*. **2**

5. (a) (i) State **two** hardware characteristics which could be used to compare a desktop computer and a network server.

   (ii) Use these characteristics to distinguish between a desktop computer and a network server. **3**

   (b) Describe **one** function which may be provided by a network operating system in addition to the standard functions of an operating system. **1**

6. State **two** functions of a peripheral device *interface* in a computer system. **2**

7. The software development process begins with the *analysis* stage and finishes with *maintenance*.

   (a) What is the purpose of the analysis stage? **1**

   (b) Name the document produced as a result of the analysis stage. **1**

   (c) There are **three** different types of maintenance which can be carried out on a piece of software once it is distributed. Name and describe each type. **3**

SECTION I (continued)

Marks

8. *Module libraries* are often used by programmers when they develop software.

    (a) What is a module library? **1**

    (b) State **two** features which make modules *portable*. **1**

    (c) Well-designed modules should be *robust* and *fit for purpose*.

    Explain each of these terms. **2**

9. A school library has just bought a program to record book loans. One of the program's modules asks for the name of a book and returns the name of the pupil who has borrowed it. Which **one** of the following algorithms is most likely to be used in this module?

    - Find minimum value
    - Linear search
    - Counting occurrences
    - Input validation **1**

10. Describe **two** features of a structured listing. **2**

11. Parameter passing is one way of controlling the flow of data between procedures. Parameters may be *passed by value* or *passed by reference*.

    Explain what is meant by the term "passed by value" in relation to parameters. **1**

12. The elimination of errors is a very important part of the software development process. *Syntax errors* and *logic errors* are two types of error which may occur.

    Use code from a programming environment with which you are familiar to illustrate **one** example of a syntax error and **one** example of a logic error. **2**

    (30)

[END OF SECTION I]

[Turn over

SECTION II

Attempt FOUR questions in this section

Question 13 and Question 14
and <u>either</u> Question 15 <u>or</u> Question 16
and <u>either</u> Question 17 <u>or</u> Question 18

Marks

13. The following diagram shows the basic design of a central processing unit. It has a 24-bit address bus and a 16-bit data bus.

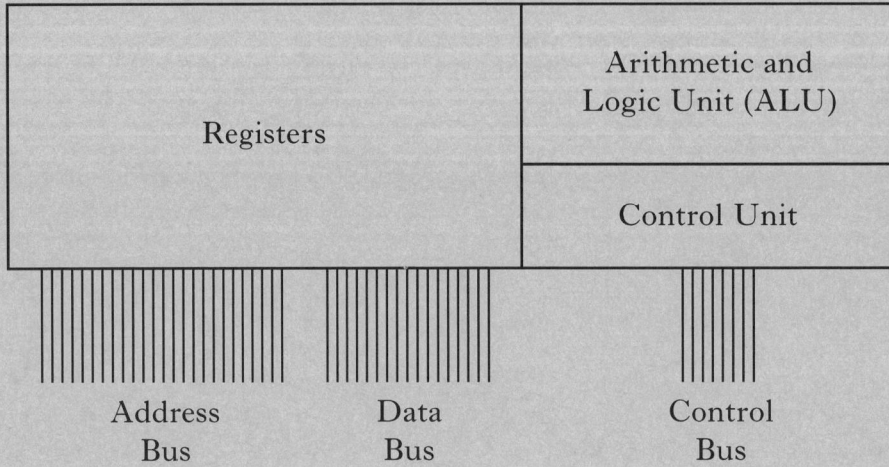

(a) A processor can be considered to be made up of **three** components: the *Arithmetic and Logic Unit (ALU)*, the *Control Unit* and *registers*.

Describe the purpose of each of these components. **3**

(b) If a processor needs an instruction from memory, a read operation is carried out. Describe the steps of the *memory read* operation with reference to the processor, memory and buses. **3**

(c) *Throughput* is one way of measuring a computer's processing power.

Describe **two** developments in the internal organisation of computers which have increased throughput. **2**

(d) Calculate the maximum amount of addressable memory which the above processor could access.

Express your answer in appropriate units. **2**

SECTION II (continued)

Marks

14. Software has to be developed for a business which will allow the automatic processing of wages. A programmer has designed a structure chart as part of the design stage of the software development process.

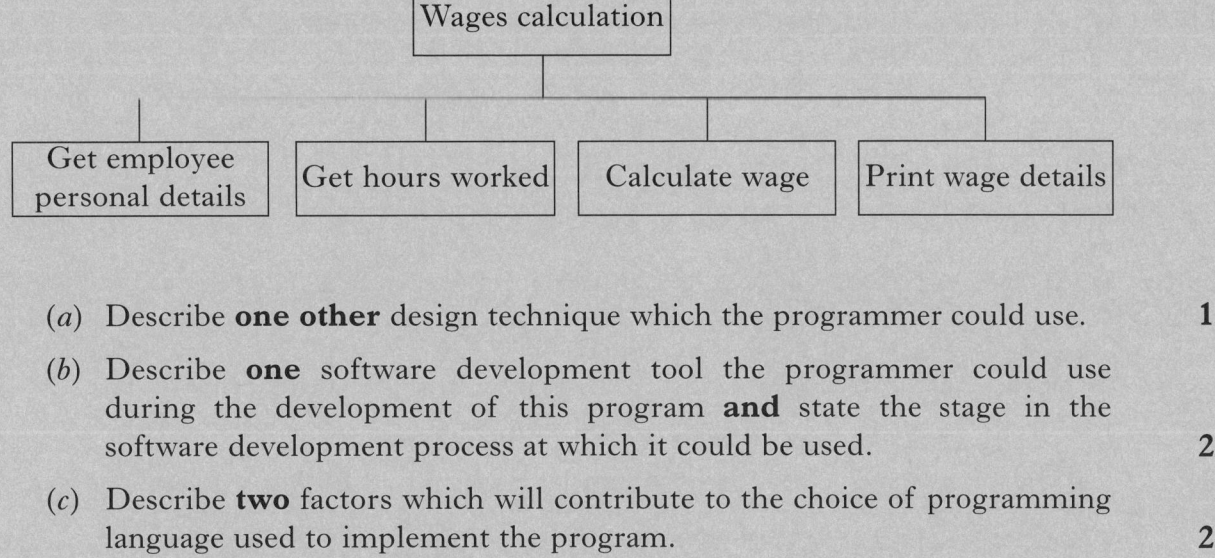

(a) Describe **one other** design technique which the programmer could use. **1**

(b) Describe **one** software development tool the programmer could use during the development of this program **and** state the stage in the software development process at which it could be used. **2**

(c) Describe **two** factors which will contribute to the choice of programming language used to implement the program. **2**

(d) Describe **two** methods the programmer could use in order to make the program readable. **2**

(e) For the "Get hours worked" procedure, give **three** items of test data the programmer could use to test this procedure fully.

Give **one** reason for **each** of your choices. **3**

[Turn over

SECTION II (continued)

Attempt either Question 15 or Question 16

15. Kingsland Drive Youth Club has decided to set up a computer system so that they can send regular newsletters to members, and keep an up-to-date list of members' details and subscriptions.

(a) List **three** types of application software they may need and describe the purpose of each type in this situation. **2**

(b) Articles for the newsletter will be provided in electronic form by members. Explain the importance of *data standards* in this situation. **2**

(c) *Input validation* is a feature provided by some application packages.

Describe how the club could use application software to validate members' details as they are entered. **1**

(d) The newsletter will contain pictures of members of the club. There is not enough money to buy both a digital camera and a scanner.

Which one would you recommend? Justify your answer, giving **two** advantages of your recommendation. **2**

(e) The club decides to buy a software package which includes a *scripting language*.

(i) What is meant by the term "scripting language"?

(ii) Describe a situation where the use of a scripting language would be helpful to the youth club. **3**

SECTION II (continued)

Marks

16. A home computer system is advertised as having a standard operating system, a selection of utility programs and some additional bundled software.

(a) Describe **three** functions of a standard operating system. **2**

(b) Describe **two** types of utility program which might be included. **2**

(c) In addition to an internal 20 Gb hard disc drive, a 1·4 Mb floppy disc drive and a 48-speed CD-ROM drive, the buyer can specify one additional storage device.

  (i) Name **one** other storage device which could be useful to a home user.

  (ii) Describe a situation in which this device would be necessary.

  Justify your answer. **2**

(d) Among the bundled software, the user finds an "intelligent chess tutor". Name a programming language suitable for developing programs which show "intelligence" and describe how this language differs from a procedural language. **2**

(e) Explain **why** a program developer may use both an interpreter and a compiler in the development of a piece of software. **2**

[Turn over

SECTION II (continued)

Attempt either Question 17 or Question 18

17. A program has been written to process a list of grades obtained by all pupils in Scotland who sat an examination. Grades are integers from 1 to 7 where 1 is the highest grade and 7 is the lowest. One of the program's functions is to count the number of pupils who obtained a grade 3, 4, 5 or 6.

A procedure is being written to carry out this function.

Here is a description of the procedure.

procedure to count number of pupils obtaining grades in a specified range

input parameters:	upper_grade, lower_grade, list_of_grades
output parameter:	number_of_pupils
process:	the procedure will count the number of grades which are between upper_grade and lower_grade inclusive.

Marks

(a) Describe **two** advantages of using *modularity* within programs. **2**

(b) Why does the procedure use the parameters "upper_grade" and "lower_grade" rather than using the numbers "3" and "6"? **1**

(c) (i) The parameters "upper_grade" and "lower_grade" could be defined as type integer or real.

Give **two** reasons why it would be better to define them as integer rather than real.

(ii) What data structure could be used to store the list of grades? **3**

(d) Describe a *complex condition* which this procedure will need to use to identify the grades which are to be counted. **2**

(e) The number of grades in the list is not known in advance.

Describe how a programmer can ensure that all grades are read and processed. You may illustrate your answer with pseudocode, or another design notation, or actual code from a programming language with which you are familiar. **2**

Marks

SECTION II (continued)

18. A program is being written to analyse the number of road traffic accidents in six areas of Scotland. The names of the areas and the number of accidents are stored in two separate arrays. One of the program's functions is to find the area with the highest number of accidents.

Here is a possible algorithm for this part of the program.

find area with highest number of accidents

1 find position of maximum number in accidents array

2 print name from corresponding position in area array

(a) The design of the *user interface* is an important part of software design.

Describe **two** characteristics of a good user interface. **2**

(b) Step 1 requires **two** parameters. Identify these parameters and state their data types and methods of parameter passing. **2**

(c) Give **one** example of a possible use of a local variable in step 1 and explain why it should be a local variable rather than a global variable. **2**

(d) Step 1 will require an *iteration* control structure and a *selection* control structure.

  (i) Describe **two** control structures which could be used.

  (ii) Show how these structures would be used to find the position of the maximum number in the accidents array. You may use pseudocode or another design notation or code from a programming language with which you are familiar. **4**

[*END OF SECTION II*]

[**Turn over**

SECTION III

Attempt ONE sub-section of Section III

Part A	Artificial Intelligence	Page 12	Questions 19 to 22
Part B	Computer Networking	Page 16	Questions 23 to 26
Part C	Computer Programming	Page 19	Questions 27 to 30
Part D	Multimedia Technology	Page 23	Questions 31 to 34

For the sub-section chosen, attempt three questions

the <u>first two</u> questions and <u>either</u> the third question <u>or</u> the fourth question.

[Turn over

SECTION III

Part A—Artificial Intelligence

**Attempt Question 19 and Question 20
and either Question 21 or Question 22**

Marks

19. Tony Wilson is a Countryside Ranger involved with the protection of endangered species in Scotland. He has asked Dr Natalie Ridge, a computer specialist, to help him create an expert system, called BatSearch, to help local volunteer groups learn how to identify seven species of bat in Scotland.

    (a) The first phase in the creation of the expert system involves Tony telling Dr Ridge how to identify Scottish bats.

     (i) Tony is the domain expert. Identify the role Dr Ridge is playing.

     (ii) Why are both Tony and Dr Ridge required at the *analysis* stage?   **3**

    (b) An expert system consists of three distinct components.

    The *user interface* is one of them.

    Name and describe the purpose of the **other two** components.   **3**

    (c) Dr Ridge asks if Tony would like to include *justification of reasoning*. Tony agrees that this would be useful. He also tells her to add a warning that it is against the law to handle live bats or to enter a roost unless you have a licence to do so.

     (i) What is meant by "justification of reasoning"?

     (ii) Why is this justification useful to the user of BatSearch?

     (iii) Explain why the information about handling live bats must be included as part of the system.   **3**

    (d) At what later stage in the development process is Tony involved?

    Give a reason for your answer.   **1**

SECTION III

Part A—Artificial Intelligence (continued)

20. Natural language processing is a fast growing area in artificial intelligence. Below is part of a program which is used to analyse sentence structure in order to work out what the sentence means. The program is written in a *declarative language* which uses *depth first search*.

    ```
    1   noun (badger)              badger is a noun
    2   noun (fox)
    3   noun (otter)

    4   verb (sees)                sees is a verb
    5   verb (jumps)
    6   verb (meets)

    7   adjective (brown)          brown is an adjective
    8   adjective (quick)
    9   adjective (lazy)

    10  sentence (A B C) if
          noun (A) and             A sentence is a noun
          verb (B) and             followed by a verb
          noun (C)                 followed by a noun
    ```

    (a) (i) What would be the output from the following query?

    ?sentence (badger meets otter)

    (ii) Explain how the system would evaluate the query. **3**

    (b) The first solution for the query ?sentence (A sees C) is

    A = badger, C = badger.

    (i) What is the **second** solution?

    (ii) Describe how you would alter the sentence rule so that the nouns are always different and sentences like **"badger sees badger"** are no longer valid. **3**

    (c) Using the syntax above, write a rule called "complex_sentence" which would allow a sentence such as:

    "lazy badger meets brown fox". **2**

    (d) What difficulties would be encountered if the system were to be expanded to analyse all possible English sentences? **2**

[Turn over

SECTION III

Part A—Artificial Intelligence (continued)

Attempt either Question 21 or Question 22

21. Artificial Intelligence (AI) programs are often used in problem solving situations where the number of possible outcomes is large. One such area is in the design of processors. For example, a program might search through every possible design, examining each in turn to see which is the most efficient.

    (a) Two common search methods are *depth-first* and *breadth-first*. Describe how these search methods differ in their execution.

    You may use a diagram to illustrate your answer. **3**

    (b) A well-chosen *heuristic* might be used to make the search more efficient.

    (i) Explain the term "heuristic".

    (ii) How would a well-chosen heuristic aid efficiency? **2**

    AI might also have a role to play in the automated manufacture of circuit boards, through the use of visual recognition systems.

    (c) (i) Describe how the introduction of such a system might aid the manufacturing process. **3**

    (ii) Give **one** financial advantage of introducing such a system.

    (d) The recognition system could be implemented in one of two ways:

    - using a *procedural language* like C
    - using a *declarative language* like Prolog or Lisp.

    Choose **one** of these development environments and give **one** advantage and **one** disadvantage of your choice compared to the alternative environment. **2**

SECTION III

Part A—Artificial Intelligence (continued)

22. Recent advances in the use of *certainty factors* have allowed developers to mimic the thought processes of humans more closely.

    (a) Explain what is meant by "certainty factors". **1**

    (b) (i) Give a brief description of a medical or industrial application where certainty factors may be used to improve expert systems.

    (ii) Describe a possible legal implication which might arise from the use of this type of application. **3**

    (c) Describe the effects upon the field of Artificial Intelligence (AI) of **two** technological advances in hardware over the past two decades. Your answer should clearly show how these advances have aided the development of AI. **2**

    (d) One area of research is *computer vision*. Describe **two** aspects of human vision which are difficult to replicate in a computer vision system. **2**

    (e) Explain in detail how a neural network that is used in recognising postcodes can improve in performance over time. **2**

[END OF SECTION III PART A]

SECTION III

Part B—Computer Networking

**Attempt Question 23 and Question 24
and either Question 25 or Question 26**

Marks

23. Ettrickbank College is planning the installation of 200 new computer workstations. Unlike its original suite of computers, these will be networked.

    (a) Describe **one** economic factor and **one** technical factor which have led to the development of computer networking. **2**

    (b) In addition to the 200 workstations, three servers will be required. One of these will be a *fileserver*.

       (i) Name **two** other types of server which are likely to be needed.

       (ii) Describe the function of each type. **2**

    (c) State whether the network described above is a *peer-to-peer* or a *client-server* network. Justify your answer. **1**

    (d) Explain **how** the security of user files may be ensured in this network. **2**

    (e) (i) Explain **why** a backup strategy is necessary for this network.

       (ii) Describe a suitable backup strategy, and explain how it could be implemented. **3**

24. (a) Describe the purpose of each of the following devices in networking:

       (i) a *repeater*

       (ii) a *bridge*

       (iii) a *router*. **3**

    (b) International *protocols*, such as FTP and SMTP, are vital for successful networking.

       (i) Describe the purpose of each of these protocols.

       (ii) Explain why international protocols are required. **3**

    (c) A self-employed plumber has created a simple Web site advertising his services. He wants his site to "go live" on the Internet. Two possible URLs for the site are:

    www.billtheplumber.co.uk, or

    www.freewebservice.com/users/pages/billtheplumber.

    Describe **one** advantage and **one** disadvantage of each URL. **2**

    (d) Describe how facilities provided by the Internet could:

       (i) benefit a small business such as a self-employed plumber

       (ii) cause difficulties for a small business. **2**

SECTION III

Part B—Computer Networking (continued)

Answer **either** Question 25 **or** Question 26

25. Five computers have been donated to Millside Library for public use.

    (a) Describe **two** advantages of networking these computers within the library. **2**

    (b) State **one** additional item of hardware and **one** additional item of software which will need to be installed in the stand-alone computers if they are to be networked. Describe the purpose of each item. **2**

    (c) A star topology has been chosen for the network.

    (i) State **one** advantage of a star topology compared with a bus topology.

    (ii) What **additional** item of hardware will be required to implement a star network? Explain why this will be necessary.

    (iii) Name **two** types of cabling which may be used in networking.

    Which one would you recommend to connect the computers within the library? Give a reason for your choice. **4**

    (d) It is proposed to connect Millside Library's network to Millside High School's network.

    (i) Why is this described as an *internetwork* rather than a wide area network?

    (ii) Describe **one** benefit this could bring to the library users and **one** benefit it could bring to the school pupils. **2**

[Turn over

SECTION III

Part B—Computer Networking (continued)

26. ScotWest Bank plc has 20 branches located throughout Scotland and a head office in Glasgow. Each branch has a local area network (LAN), and the branches and head office are connected by a wide area network (WAN).

(a) Distinguish between a LAN and a WAN in terms of

  (i) bandwidth

  (ii) transmission media.   **2**

(b) Describe **two** ways of ensuring security when financial data is being transferred between a branch and head office.   **2**

(c) Explain how the increased use of computer networks in the banking industry has brought benefits to:

  (i) customers

  (ii) staff.   **2**

(d) As a result of increased use of networking, the bank has long-term plans to close many of its branches. Customers complain that they will miss the opportunity to talk "face to face" with bank staff.

  (i) Describe a technological solution to this difficulty.

  (ii) Describe the specific hardware and software each customer would require (in **addition** to a computer) to implement your solution.   **4**

[*END OF SECTION III PART B*]

SECTION III

Part C—Computer Programming

**Attempt Question 27 and Question 28
and either Question 29 or Question 30**

Marks

27. The following names have been stored in an array as part of a personal organiser program which is being developed by a team of programmers.

    John
    Mary
    Alan
    Peter
    Gordon

The programmers want to add a search feature to the program so that a person's name can be found quickly.

It has been decided that a *binary search* will be used.

(a) (i) What would need to be done to the list of names once a *binary search* has been chosen?

    (ii) Why is this necessary?   2

(b) State **three** data items which would be required in addition to the list of names to implement the *binary search algorithm* and explain how these data items are used in the algorithm.   3

(c) Use the list of numbers

    12, 15, 19, 23, 29

to compare the performance of the *binary search algorithm* with the *linear search algorithm* when the number 23 is to be found.   2

(d) In what circumstances would the *linear search algorithm* out-perform the *binary search algorithm*? Explain your answer.   2

(e) Explain why the efficiency of the search algorithm is important if the program is to be used on a palmtop computer.   1

[Turn over

SECTION III

Part C—Computer Programming (continued)

28. Fruitbat Software have been asked to implement a new set of card games. The cards are each to be represented by a code as shown below:

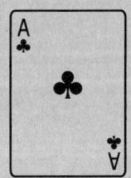
Ace of Clubs is AC

Ten of Diamonds is 10 D

King of Spades is KS

Five of Hearts is 5H

(a) One of the games involves dealing 13 cards into a separate pile to be used during the game. This pile is called the "bank".

The programmer has decided to use an *array* to represent the bank.

  (i) What **size** and **type** of array should be used for the bank?

  (ii) State **two** advantages of holding the bank using an array rather than as a series of variables. **3**

(b) Two complex data structures available to the programmer are a *stack* and a *queue*. Explain the difference between these two structures. **2**

(c) The array operates as a *stack*. As the game is played, cards are removed from the bank. When a card is removed from the bank, its code is *popped* from the top of the *stack*.

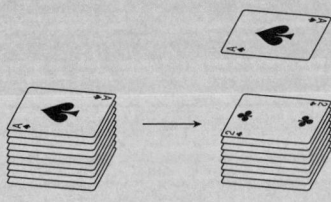
Card is popped

Describe, in pseudocode or otherwise, the process of popping a card from the stack. **3**

(d) One of the required features of the new software is the ability to save the bank to file. Describe, in pseudocode or otherwise, the process of saving the bank into a file. **2**

Marks

SECTION III

Part C—Computer Programming (continued)

Answer **either** Question 29 **or** Question 30

29. At a canoe slalom event, competitors are timed on a section of river. They set off at two minute intervals. At the finishing line, a judge writes down each competitor's name, bib number, time and penalty points. After three competitors have completed the course, the judge's notes look like this:

Name	Bib number	Time (seconds)	Penalty points
J Ashcroft	273	127·4	15
N Khan	185	153·2	10
S Buchanan	99	187·4	45

The judge is to be provided with a laptop computer running a specially designed program. This will allow each competitor's name, bib number, time and penalties to be entered as they finish, and stored in a file on disc.

(a) Name **two** file operations which will be required by the program, and explain why they are needed. **2**

(b) Each competitor's results are stored as a *record* in the file. Describe, in detail, a suitable record structure for this data. **2**

(c) Once all the results have been stored, they must be sorted into ascending order of the competitor's time.

　(i) Name **one** sort algorithm which could be used.

　(ii) Describe how this sort algorithm works. You may use a diagram, pseudocode or any other suitable form. **3**

(d) Name **one other** sort algorithm, and compare it with the one chosen in (c) in terms of:

　(i) use of memory

　(ii) use of processor time. **2**

(e) Explain why the three sets of results given in the table above would be inadequate test data to test this program. **1**

[Turn over

SECTION III

Part C—Computer Programming (continued)

30. The weather station at Loch Dubh has recorded the level of monthly rainfall in the area for 20 years from 1980 to 1999.

Here is a sample of the data for the years 1990 and 1991.

Year	Jan	Feb	Mar	Apr	May	Jun	Jul	Aug	Sept	Oct	Nov	Dec
.	.	.	.	.	.	.	.	.	.	.	.	.
.	.	.	.	.	.	.	.	.	.	.	.	.
1990	10·3	9·3	9·8	15·1	13·4	4·1	2·3	4·3	6·7	6·8	9·8	7·6
1991	11·3	21·1	5·8	12·7	16·3	7·4	3·2	4·6	7·1	7·2	8·6	10·3
.	.	.	.	.	.	.	.	.	.	.	.	.
.	.	.	.	.	.	.	.	.	.	.	.	.

Rainfall (in cm)

Marks

(a) Define a two dimensional array to store **all** of the data. **1**

(b) The staff at the weather station want to know how many times the rainfall was greater than 10 cm.

  (i) Describe, using pseudocode or otherwise, how the number of months when the rainfall was over 10 cm could be calculated for a single year.

  (ii) Describe the changes which would need to be made to the algorithm to perform this calculation for the 20 year period. **4**

(c) The maximum monthly rainfall for each year has to be found.

  Describe how this could be done for each year using a one-dimensional array to store the results. **3**

(d) The weather station wants to record the monthly rainfall for the next 20 years and continue making comparisons between months.

  Describe **two** specific examples of *perfective maintenance* which would need to be made to the program. **2**

[*END OF SECTION III PART C*]

SECTION III

Part D—Multimedia Technology

**Attempt Question 31 and Question 32
and <u>either</u> Question 33 <u>or</u> Question 34**

Marks

31. Over the last 20 years there has been a huge increase in the development of multimedia related hardware and software. *Hypermedia* and *Computer Based Training* are both applications of multimedia technology.

   (a) Hypermedia systems have developed from *hypertext* systems.

   (i) Describe **one** feature common to both systems.

   (ii) Describe **one** extra feature you would expect to find in a hypermedia system.   **2**

   (b) Many businesses are now using Computer Based Training instead of traditional training methods.

   (i) Describe a situation where Computer Based Training would be useful.

   (ii) Describe **one** advantage of using Computer Based Training rather than traditional training methods in this situation.   **2**

   (c) A hardware specification is being developed for a Computer Based Training system.

   (i) Describe **two** advantages of using a DVD instead of a CD-ROM in this situation.

   (ii) Describe **two** characteristics of display hardware and explain how they will affect the quality of the Computer Based Training presentation.

   (iii) The development team has been told that the budget will allow either a faster processor or additional RAM to be purchased. Which upgrade would you recommend? Justify your answer.   **6**

[*Turn over*

SECTION III

Part D—Multimedia Technology (continued)

Marks

32. A multimedia designer has been employed to create a multimedia project for a local bus company. The designer has created a design of the home page below.

```
+-------------------+-------------------------------+
| Video of company  |       Company's logo          |
| buses in action   +-------------------------------+
|                   | Description of bus routes     |
|                   | and bus timetables with       |
|                   | hyperlinks to other pages for |
|                   | further information           |
+-------------------+-------------------------------+
```

(a) The designer begins by making a *storyboard* of the whole multimedia presentation.

What is a storyboard and how will it help the implementation of the presentation? **2**

(b) The designer is aware that the multimedia pages could be developed using either an *icon-based* or a *script-based* package.

Which one would you recommend to the designer? Explain your choice. **2**

(c) In addition to a computer system, name **two** items of hardware the designer may have to use to produce this home page and **describe the function** of **each** item. **2**

(d) The designer has decided that the home page should include a feature which enables the user to hear the bus times and routes.

Explain how this could be done. Your explanation should include a description of any software and hardware which will be required. **3**

(e) Explain the importance of MPC standards when designing multimedia presentations. **1**

SECTION III

Part D—Multimedia Technology (continued)

Answer **either** Question 33 **or** Question 34

33. A small photography business has created a presentation of its best photographs. These photographs can be viewed on the computers in the company's shops.

    (a) Name **two** possible hardware devices which could capture the photographs. Describe how each device would be used. **2**

    (b) There are different techniques which may be used to store photographs.

      (i) Explain the difference between *lossy* and *lossless* compression.

      (ii) Name **two** standard file formats which could be used to store the photographs. Which one would you recommend? Justify your answer. **3**

    (c) One of the services provided by the company is the ability to "enhance" customers' photographs.

    Describe **three** features of graphic manipulation software which the company might use to provide this service. **3**

    (d) The company now wishes to create a magazine of its best photographs to send to customers. Instead of using a word processing package they decide to use a desk top publishing package.

    Describe **two** advantages of using a desk top publishing package rather than a word processing package to produce the magazine. **2**

34. Using synthesised music is an important part of the popular music industry today.

    (a) Describe how the Musical Instrument Digital Interface (MIDI) has contributed to this development. **2**

    (b) Describe the difference between *Frequency Modulation* and *Wave Table Synthesis*. **2**

    (c) *Compression* and *sampling rates* are important factors in audio processing.

      (i) Describe what is meant by the terms "compression" and "sampling rate".

      (ii) Name and describe **two** different audio file formats.

      (iii) Explain why it is necessary to use a sampling rate which is neither too low nor too high when recording sound. **6**

[*END OF SECTION III PART D*]

[*END OF QUESTION PAPER*]

[BLANK PAGE]

2003 HIGHER

X017/301

NATIONAL
QUALIFICATIONS
2003

THURSDAY, 22 MAY
1.00 PM – 3.30 PM

COMPUTING
HIGHER

Attempt **all** questions in Section I.

Attempt **four** questions in Section II

    Question 14 and Question 15
    and **either** Question 16 **or** Question 17
    and **either** Question 18 **or** Question 19

Attempt **one** sub-section of Section III.

Part A	Artificial Intelligence	Page 12	Questions 20 to 23
Part B	Computer Networking	Page 15	Questions 24 to 27
Part C	Computer Programming	Page 17	Questions 28 to 31
Part D	Multimedia Technology	Page 21	Questions 32 to 35

For the sub-section chosen, attempt **three** questions.

The **first two** questions and **either** the third question **or** the fourth question.

Read all questions carefully.

Do not write on the question paper.

Write as neatly as possible.

SECTION I

Attempt all questions in this section

Marks

1. Describe **three** different types of software maintenance. **3**

2. During the implementation stage in any software development project, the target is to deliver code which is <u>correct</u> and <u>reliable</u>.

   Explain **both** of the underlined terms. **2**

3. When producing software, it is very important to have good design and clear documentation.

   (a) (i) Name **two** methods of representing program design.

   (ii) Give **one** advantage of **each** method. **3**

   (b) Describe **two** items of documentation that would accompany the finished software. **2**

4. *Fixed loops* and *conditional loops* are types of *iterative* control structures.

   (a) Describe a conditional loop. You may use an example from a programming language with which you are familiar. **1**

   (b) What is the difference between a fixed loop and a conditional loop? **1**

   (c) Explain the meaning of "iterative" in relation to control structures. **1**

5. A *readable* program is easier to maintain.

   (a) Explain why a readable program is easier to maintain. **1**

   (b) State **two** techniques that programmers could use to make their programs more readable. **1**

6. (a) What feature of computer architecture determines *word size*? **1**

   (b) Explain how word size affects system performance. **1**

7. The processor and memory are linked by the *address*, *data* and *control buses*.

   Give **two** examples of the use of the control bus. **1**

8. A company logo has been created in both *vector* and *bit-mapped* graphics packages. Describe **two** actions which could be carried out on the "vector graphic" but not on the "bit-mapped graphic". **2**

9. *Signed-bit* and *two's complement* are two ways of storing binary integers. Give **two** advantages of using two's complement rather than signed-bit. **2**

SECTION I (continued)

Marks

10. (a) (i) State **one** network topology that could be used for a local area network.

    (ii) Draw a labelled diagram of this topology. **1**

    (b) What would be the result of channel failure in your chosen topology? **1**

11. State **one** similarity and **one** difference between *scripting* and *procedural* programming languages. **2**

12. *Resolution* and *capacity* are important features of digital cameras.

    (a) Explain the terms "resolution" and "capacity" in relation to digital cameras. **1**

    (b) Describe how the resolution of a digital camera affects its capacity. **1**

13. Standard file formats are often used to transfer data between applications packages of the same type.

    Choose **two** different types of application package and state **one** standard file format for each. **2**

    (30)

[END OF SECTION I]

[Turn over

SECTION II

Attempt FOUR questions in this section

Question 14 and Question 15
and **either** Question 16 **or** Question 17
and **either** Question 18 **or** Question 19

Marks

14. Most computers are still based on the system proposed by John von Neumann.

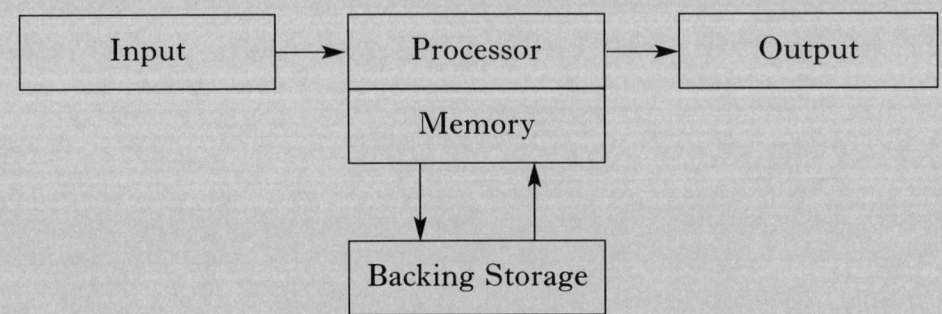

- (a) (i) Explain how memory is organised so that data can be stored and retrieved by the processor.

    (ii) Explain the importance of the *memory management* function of the operating system.

- (b) *Registers* are one component of the processor.

    (i) Explain how the number of registers can affect system performance.

    (ii) Name **one** other component of the processor and describe its function.

- (c) Different types of memory can be used within a computer system such as *ROM*, *RAM*, *SRAM* and *DRAM*.

    (i) Explain why *maintainability* of ROM-based software could pose problems.

    (ii) Describe **one** solution to this problem not involving the use of RAM.

    (iii) Describe **one** advantage and **one** disadvantage of using DRAM instead of SRAM other than cost.

- (d) A computer system with a microprocessor which has a 24-bit data bus and a 32-bit address bus is sold with 1 Gb of addressable memory. What is the maximum amount of **additional** memory which could be added to this computer system?

    Express your answer using appropriate units.

2

2

4

2

SECTION II (continued)

Marks

15. A software company has been asked to create a piece of software to help an employment agency match various jobs with prospective employees. The software company carries out an analysis on how the agency currently performs this task.

(a) Describe **one** method that the software company might have used to analyse the agency's current system. **1**

The software will store the responses of applicants to a number of standard questions. The applicants' responses are whole numbers in the range 1 to 5.

(b) The set of responses given by the applicants must be held during processing. These are held in an *array of integers*. Give **two** reasons why an array has been chosen to hold the responses. **2**

(c) When the array is searched, the module responsible returns the location of where the item is found. The search item can be passed as a parameter either *by reference* or *by value*.

   (i) Explain the terms "pass by reference" and "pass by value".

   (ii) Which is more appropriate for passing the search item? Justify your choice. **3**

(d) The software development team could have chosen to implement the program in a **declarative** language.

Explain why they might have considered this approach. **2**

(e) Good documentation should be developed both at the *implementation* stage and at the *testing* stage of the software development process.

Describe how documentation from **each** of these stages can benefit *maintainability*. **2**

[Turn over

Marks

SECTION II (continued)

Attempt either Question 16 or Question 17

16. A publishing business uses a range of computer systems, software and peripherals to produce its newspapers and magazines.

    (a) Name a type of software application it could choose for creating a newspaper and give **one** reason for your choice. **1**

    (b) A high resolution scanner is used to capture photographs onto a computer.

    (i) Describe **two** hardware features of a scanner, other than resolution.

    (ii) Calculate how much storage would be required for a 6 ↔ 4 inch photograph scanned at 600 dpi using 256 colours.

    Express your answer in appropriate units. **4**

    (c) (i) The business wants to equip its journalists with either laptop or palmtop computers. Which computer system would you recommend? Give **one hardware** and **one software** reason for your choice.

    (ii) Describe how the *user interface* of your recommended system could benefit the journalist. **3**

    (d) The business decides to invest in a piece of software which will allow readers to search for past news stories using keywords. Give **one** advantage and **one** disadvantage to the software house of using a general-purpose database package to create this software rather than creating a specialised software package. **2**

SECTION II (continued)

Marks

17. Panes 2001 is a stand-alone operating system. It boasts many features such as:
    - Plug and play
    - Graphical user interface
    - Utility software
    - Multimedia features.

    (a) Why does a computer require an operating system? **1**

    (b) What is *utility software*? Describe **one** utility which may be provided with Panes 2001. **2**

    (c) In order to use multimedia elements (such as text, graphics, video and sound), *standard file formats* have to be used by the software.

    Why are standard file formats necessary? **1**

    (d) One of the system requirements for Panes 2001 is that it requires 256 Mb of RAM. Describe **two** other **hardware** requirements which may be necessary for a computer to run an operating system such as Panes 2001. **2**

    (e) An upgrade to Panes 2001 is to include many extra features including video manipulation and voice recognition.

    (i) Explain how the use of modular programming in Panes 2001 could benefit the coding of these new features.

    (ii) Describe **two** methods that programmers could use at the testing stage to ensure that the upgrade is free from errors. **4**

[Turn over

SECTION II (continued)

Attempt either Question 18 or Question 19

18. The Scottish Tree Foundation has commissioned a piece of software to be written to gather information for a national survey of trees in Scotland. The prototypes of two styles of user interface are shown below.

    Interface A

    Please enter tree name . . .
    ?|

    Interface B

    Please choose the tree name from the list and press OK   OK

    Oak, Black
    Oak, Holm
    Oak, Sessile
    Pear, Common
    Pear, Willow-leaved

    Using this program, data is gathered and output to a text file for processing later.

    (a) Describe **each** of the interfaces in terms of *robustness, ease of data entry* and *efficiency of computer resources*. **3**

    (b) Describe **two** features of an *event driven* language which would make it easier to implement Interface B compared with using a procedural language. **2**

    (c) The software must be run on a number of different computer systems. Describe **two** ways in which the software company could make the program *portable*. **2**

    (d) It is suggested that the time required to develop the program might be reduced by the use of a module library.

    How might the use of a *module library* accelerate the development process? **1**

    (e) One module of the program will take a tree name from the user and will count all occurrences of that name in the current list of trees. The module will return the number of times the name appears in the list or zero if the name is not found. Using pseudocode or otherwise, write a detailed algorithm for this process. **2**

SECTION II (continued)

Marks

19. A large suite of software consisting of separate modules is being developed by several programming teams. A number of stages are gone through to ensure that these modules will fit together properly.

   (a) Individual programmers can take steps during the writing of these modules that will make the modules fit together more easily. A program can be made more *robust* by using local variables instead of global variables where possible.

   (i) Explain the difference between *global variables* and *local variables*.

   (ii) How would the use of local variables contribute to the "robustness" of the software? **3**

   (b) The type of programming language used for software implementation must be decided at an early stage in the design process.

   Describe **three** factors, other than the expertise of the programmers, which will affect the final choice of language for the implementation. **3**

   The software is able to have several windows open at once. The program holds a list of the names of all open windows in an appropriate data structure.

   (c) What type of data structure is being used to hold the names? Your answer should state the **full** data type of the data structure. **1**

   When a window is selected, a software module finds the position of that window in the list. For example, when the user clicks on a window, the module checks the list and returns its position in the list.

   (d) Use pseudocode, or another design notation of your choice, to fully describe the process of identifying the position of the name in the list. **2**

   (e) When the software is handling the window selection process described above, it communicates with part of the operating system. Which part of the operating system is involved? Justify your answer. **1**

[*END OF SECTION II*]

[**Turn over**

[BLANK PAGE]

SECTION III

Attempt ONE sub-section of Section III

Part A	Artificial Intelligence	Page 12	Questions 20 to 23
Part B	Computer Networking	Page 15	Questions 24 to 27
Part C	Computer Programming	Page 17	Questions 28 to 31
Part D	Multimedia Technology	Page 21	Questions 32 to 35

For the sub-section chosen, attempt three questions

the <u>first two</u> questions and <u>either</u> the third question <u>or</u> the fourth question.

[Turn over

SECTION III

Part A—Artificial Intelligence

**Attempt Question 20 and Question 21
and either Question 22 or Question 23**

20. (a) MYCIN is an expert system which is used for medical diagnosis. It has been in use for over three decades and during this time it has been continually improved.

    (i) Describe **two** advances in **hardware** which have contributed to its improvement over this time.

    (ii) Describe **one** legal implication of using such expert systems and suggest how a good explanatory interface within an expert system could help to prevent such problems.

    (iii) Suggest **two** reasons why expert systems such as MYCIN are useful even though there may be several human experts in various medical centres around the world. **6**

    (b) Knowledge acquisition is an important stage in the development of an expert system. Explain why knowledge acquisition is an *iterative* process. **2**

    (c) Expert systems is one area of current artificial intelligence (AI) research. Others include *natural language processing* and *computer vision*. Suggest **two** reasons why there is such a large number of areas for research within the field of AI. **2**

SECTION III

Part A—Artificial Intelligence (continued)

21. The following knowledge base summarises the management structure of a small company.

1	is_manager_of(friedland,bennett)	Friedland is Bennett's manager
2	is_manager_of(friedland,brown)	
3	is_manager_of(friedland,everson)	
4	is_manager_of(grainger,friedland)	
5	is_manager_of(grainger,hill)	
6	is_manager_of(hill,backley)	
7	is_manager_of(hill,foster)	
8	male(everson)	
9	male(foster)	
10	male(grainger)	
11	male(hill)	
12	female(X) if not male(X)	X is female if X is not male
13	boss(X,Y) if is_manager_of(X,Y)	X is Y's boss if X is Y's manager
14	boss(X,Y) if is_manager_of(X,Z) and boss(Z,Y)	X is Y's boss if X is the manager of Z and Z is Y's boss

    (a) (i) What would be the result of the following query?

    ?male(macdonald)

    (ii) In terms of this knowledge base, what problem is there with this result? **2**

    (b) Trace the solution to the query:

    ?female(friedland) **2**

    (c) Write a complex query to find out which female employees have Grainger as their boss. **2**

    (d) Two people are in the same department if they have the same immediate manager. Design a rule to show this. **2**

    (e) (i) Explain why the rules in lines 13 and 14 are both required.

    (ii) Why must they appear in the order shown? **2**

[Turn over

SECTION III

Part A—Artificial Intelligence (continued)

Attempt either Question 22 or Question 23

22. (a) Give **two** reasons why simple game playing was an important part of early artificial intelligence research. **2**

  (b) A computer has been programmed to play noughts and crosses against a human opponent. The human opponent does not know whether he is playing against a computer or another human. He has been asked to work out which it is.

  Why would it be difficult for a human player to decide whether he was playing against a computer or another human? **2**

  (c) A robot is being programmed to solve a jigsaw puzzle using computer vision techniques.

   (i) Describe **two** difficulties when using computer vision in this context.

   (ii) Suggest how the use of a simple *heuristic* may be applied to the computer vision algorithm to solve a jigsaw puzzle. **4**

  (d) State clearly how research into *pattern matching* and *parallel processing* may assist in the development of intelligent robots. **2**

23. (a) Databases and knowledge bases are both used to store information. Describe **two** ways in which they differ. **2**

  (b) Give **one** reason why the knowledge base and inference engine are separated in the traditional architecture of an expert system shell. **1**

  (c) A *domain expert* provides the knowledge which is stored in an expert system. Name **one** other person who is involved in creating an expert system and **describe** the role of this person. **1**

  (d) In many situations human experts cannot be precise about the advice that they give. They may only be able to say that their advice is very likely to be correct in a particular situation.

   (i) Describe a feature of an expert system that could help to model this type of advice.

   (ii) Describe how this feature might be used in a particular situation. **2**

  (e) Advice from an expert system can be arrived at by using either *forward chaining* or *backward chaining*.

   (i) Using a syntax with which you are familiar, give an example of a forward chaining rule and a backward chaining rule.

   (ii) For what type of problem is forward chaining best suited?

   (iii) To what type of problem is backward chaining best suited? **4**

[END OF SECTION III PART A]

SECTION III

Part B—Computer Networking

**Attempt Question 24 and Question 25
and either Question 26 or Question 27**

Marks

24. A large insurance company makes extensive use of the Internet and e-mail. The company also has computer-based networked information systems and its own intranet. Some of the company's staff have access to the entire network from home using a dial-up connection.

    (a) The company has used the *client-server* networking model rather than the *peer-to-peer* model when designing its network.

    (i) Explain the terms "peer-to-peer" and "client-server".

    (ii) Give **two** reasons why it has chosen the client-server model. **4**

    (b) Suggest **two** reasons why access to the company's network is slower from home than it is from the office. **2**

    (c) The IT Manager is worried that the company's network might be broken into by unauthorised people.

    Describe **two** ways a *firewall* could prevent unauthorised access. **2**

    (d) The dial-up server offers a "callback" facility. When an employee dials from home, the dial-up server checks their user name and password, terminates the connection and then re-establishes the link to the employee's home number.

    Give **two** reasons why this feature is used in addition to the firewall. **2**

25. A business has several large offices, one in each of the main capital cities of Europe. Each office has a local area network (LAN) of desktop computers. The company now wishes to connect all of the offices to one another, so that any computer in one office can access data which is stored on the server of another office. The TCP/IP stack is used on all of the computers.

    (a) (i) What **device** is necessary to connect the LANs?

    (ii) Give **one** reason for your choice. **2**

    (b) Describe the steps involved in the transfer of files between computers using the TCP/IP protocol. **2**

    (c) One of the company's LANs provides multimedia CD-ROM sharing. State, with reasons, **two** requirements of the LAN for this to operate satisfactorily. **2**

    (d) The business makes heavy use of printed output. Describe **two** functions provided by a *print server* to control printing. **2**

    (e) Explain how the use of TCP/IP has led to the development and growth of *intranets*. **2**

[Turn over

SECTION III

Part B—Computer Networking (continued)

Answer either Question 26 or Question 27

26. (a) It is claimed that: "computer networks create information rich and information poor individuals or societies".

Explain what is meant by this statement. **2**

(b) When downloading or using information from another country, a user may accidently break the law. Why might this cause difficulties for legal authorities across the world? **2**

(c) A method called the Domain Name System is used to construct Internet addresses. A URL is of the form:

protocol: // host_address/resource name

For each part of the URL:

   (i) describe its purpose, and

   (ii) give an example from an actual URL. **3**

(d) A major step forward in the development of the Internet was the development of *packet switching* as a data transmission method.

   (i) State **one** other data transmission method.

   (ii) Describe **two** advantages of packet switching when compared to your answer to (i). **3**

27. A team of fashion designers work in an office with computers which are connected to a local area network. They also have access to the World Wide Web. Each member of the team has a laptop and a digital camera which they use when working away from their main office.

(a) (i) Name **one** item of hardware and **one** item of software which would be needed to allow communication between the laptops and the office server.

   (ii) Describe **two** tasks that the item of **software** would carry out. **3**

(b) The team also uses video conferencing to share ideas and information when meetings in the office are not possible.

   (i) Describe **two** facilities which video conferencing makes available.

   (ii) Security is an important consideration for this company. How can the company ensure that a video conference is secure? **3**

(c) (i) Name a file format which is suitable for transmitting photographs over a typical Internet link.

   (ii) Describe **two** features of this file format which make it suitable for this purpose. **2**

(d) The fashion house transmits its designs over a wide-area-network (WAN) which conforms to the Open Systems Interconnection (OSI) model.

Name and describe **two** layers of the OSI model. **2**

[END OF SECTION III PART B]

SECTION III

Part C—Computer Programming

**Attempt Question 28 and Question 29
and <u>either</u> Question 30 <u>or</u> Question 31**

Marks

28. When a computer receives an *interrupt* signal from a peripheral requiring attention, it saves the address of the instruction that it is currently processing by *pushing* it onto a *stack*. When it has dealt with the peripheral, it *pops* the saved address for the previous task from the stack and carries on from where it stopped.

    (a) What type of data structure will be used to implement the stack? Your answer should state the **full** data type of the data structure.   1

    (b) What **two** items of data must the program hold if it is to be able to use the stack?   2

    (c) Describe the process of *pushing* an item onto a stack. You may use a diagram to illustrate your answer.   3

    (d) Another part of the software deals with holding jobs in a print queue. Jobs in this queue are carried out in order of priority. This is determined by the two digit job number allocated to the document to be printed. Jobs are held in a sorted list. Any new jobs are added to the list and the list is then re-ordered.

    Example:

    Old list: 13, 27, 39, 42

    Job number 13 is sent to the printer and the queue manager receives a new job from a user (31).

    Unsorted list: 27, 39, 42, 31
    New list: 27, 31, 39, 42

    (i) Describe, using pseudocode or otherwise, **one** method of sorting the list:

    27, 39, 42, 31.

    (ii) Describe the efficiency of your sorting algorithm in terms of the number of comparisons and memory use.   4

[Turn over

SECTION III

Part C—Computer Programming (continued)

29. A wages program is to read an alphabetical list of names and the number of hours worked from a text file. Each person's data is to be held as a pair on a single line in the file. Before the weekly wage is calculated, the data is to be read into two parallel one-dimensional arrays. The hourly rate will be held in a variable called **rate**. The calculated wages are stored in a third array before being output to the printer.

(a) The developers are worried about generating a *run-time error* whilst reading the data from the file.

  (i) Describe a "run-time error" that could occur at this stage.

  (ii) Describe a programming method, or language structure, that could be used to detect this error and so prevent the program from crashing. **3**

(b) Using pseudocode or another suitable form, show how the data is read into arrays from the text file. **3**

(c) The wages program will be implemented in a high level language. High level language programs need to be translated using either an interpreter or a compiler.

Use a loop construct from a language with which you are familiar to compare the efficiency of translation and execution using a compiler and an interpreter. **2**

(d) When an employee leaves the company, the employee's data is removed from the wages list. Describe, using an algorithm or other method, how a data pair at a given position in the arrays could be removed so that when the arrays are output back to the file there will be no blank lines.

It may be assumed that the item has been found and is held in an appropriate variable. **2**

Marks

SECTION III

Part C—Computer Programming (continued)

Answer **either** Question 30 **or** Question 31

30. Below is an extract from the datafile used by the Cree Valley Cookery Club to hold details of their 128 members. It holds the Membership Number, Member Name, Membership Class and Favourite Recipe of each member.

Membership Number	Member Name	Membership Class	Favourite Recipe
112	Seawright, D	Full	Game Pie
113	Ramsay, R	Student	Pork Casserole
114	Edeling, M	Full	Chocolate Cake
115	Lloyd, C	Full	Mushroom Pastry
116	Carrick, E	Full	Grilled Swordfish

(a) The software will report how many members of a given Membership Class are in the file. Name the standard algorithm that is used in this part of the software. **1**

During the implementation phase, programming teams refer to a detailed algorithm of the software produced by the design team. After the code is written, a *dry run* is carried out followed by *component testing* and testing of the finished product.

(b) What is the purpose of a "dry run" and how is it carried out? **1**

(c) Give **two** reasons for carrying out "component testing". **2**

(d) Explain how *trace tables* and *break points* are used in the testing process. **2**

The software searches the file on any of the fields and displays the first record it finds that matches the search item.

(e) A member's details are found with a simple *linear search* on the Member Name.

  (i) The time taken to access an individual record in the file is 0·05 seconds. How long would it take to find that the name "Cobbold, T" is **not** in the file?

  (ii) If a *binary search* was used on a file of this size, how long would it take to reach the same result for "Cobbold, T"? Show all your working.

  (iii) Explain why a *binary search* would not work on the list of records shown above. **4**

[Turn over

SECTION III

Part C—Computer Programming (continued)

31. When a product code is scanned at a stock warehouse, the scanning software performs a validity check by calculating a check digit.

The first ten digits are added together and then divided by nine. The check digit is the **remainder** after dividing by nine.

(a) The code to calculate the check digit is saved as a *library function*. What is a library function? **1**

(b) The function uses a loop to calculate the check digit. Using pseudocode, or another design notation, **fully** describe the check digit function. **3**

(c) Explain the use of a *debugger* at the implementation stage. **2**

(d) The product codes and the number of items of each product are kept in two parallel arrays as shown below.

Product Code	3542568390	8745359826	2575389925	6541212003	7437645426	8734521892
Number	150	160	145	110	250	150

(i) Explain **two** difficulties that could result from a solution using parallel arrays.

(ii) Describe an alternative to using parallel arrays for the above problem and show how this would solve one of the problems identified in (i) above. **4**

[END OF SECTION III PART C]

SECTION III

Part D—Multimedia Technology

**Attempt Question 32 and Question 33
and either Question 34 or Question 35**

Marks

32. When creating a multimedia presentation, many different types of software could be used.

    (a) (i) Describe **two** different types of **authoring software** which could be used to create a multimedia presentation.

    (ii) Describe **one** advantage of each type.   4

    (b) Both hardware and software for multimedia are subject to international standards.

    (i) Explain the purpose of MPC standards.

    (ii) Name **one** minimum **hardware** requirement for an MPC computer and explain why your choice is a necessary feature of a multimedia computer.   3

    (c) The World Wide Web allows interactive multimedia presentations to be viewed around the world. It allows users to download multimedia elements such as graphics and videos.

    (i) How have *hypertext* systems contributed to the development of the World Wide Web?

    (ii) Explain the need for *compression* when storing multimedia elements.

    (iii) Explain the legal implications of downloading media elements from the World Wide Web.   3

[Turn over

SECTION III

Part D—Multimedia Technology (continued)

Marks

33. A graphic artist uses *image processing* software to produce various artwork pieces. The artist has decided to use a bit-mapped package.

    (a) The image processing software allows the artist to edit individual pixels.

    Describe **three** other features of this type of image processing software. **3**

    (b) (i) Identify **two** file formats the artist could use to save her artwork.

    (ii) Describe **one** advantage of **each** of your formats. **3**

    (c) The artist wants to store her artwork to allow it to be distributed to prospective buyers.

    (i) What backing storage medium would you recommend? Give **two** reasons for your choice.

    (ii) A buyer has the appropriate backing storage device to read the medium from (i).

    Describe **two** possible problems a buyer could still have when trying to access the artwork. **4**

SECTION III

Part D—Multimedia Technology (continued)

Answer **either** Question 34 **or** Question 35

34. A company produces videos for various occasions such as parties and weddings. They use standard analogue video cameras. The company wishes to use a computer with video editing software to edit the videos captured by the camera.

    (a) (i) Explain how the frames stored in the camera can be captured and saved to backing storage. Your answer should include relevant hardware and software at each stage.

    (ii) How could a **digital** video camera benefit the company in this situation? **4**

    (b) Most videos are captured at 25 frames per second.

    (i) State **one** advantage and **one** disadvantage of capturing at 10 frames per second compared with capturing at 25 frames per second.

    (ii) State **one** advantage and **one** disadvantage of capturing at 50 frames per second compared with capturing at 25 frames per second. **2**

    (c) (i) Describe **two** features of video editing software.

    (ii) Describe **two hardware** requirements of a computer system which is to be used for video editing.

    Your answer must include appropriate units. **4**

35. Sound and animation are two examples of multimedia elements that can be used when creating presentations and web pages. Various file formats and compression techniques are commonly used when storing these elements.

    (a) Explain the difference between *lossy* and *lossless compression*. **1**

    (b) Scanners are now a common feature of multimedia technology to capture images and text.

    Explain, in detail, how a scanner could be used to capture text as a text file. **3**

    (c) Describe **two** different file formats which could be used to save text documents. **2**

    (d) Many multimedia presentations use sound for music, voice playback and sound effects.

    (i) Explain the difference between *sampled* sound and *synthesised* sound.

    (ii) Describe **two** functions of a basic sound card. **4**

[END OF SECTION III PART D]

[END OF QUESTION PAPER]

[BLANK PAGE]